T0327672

Trading
Basics

Trading Basics

Evolution of a Trader

THOMAS N. BULKOWSKI

WILEY

John Wiley & Sons, Inc.

Published by John Wiley & Sons, Inc., Hoboken, New Jersey.

Published simultaneously in Canada.

For general information on our other products and services or for technical support, please contact our Customer Care Department within the United States at (800) 762-2974, outside the United States at (317) 572-3993 or fax (317) 572-4002.

Wiley publishes in a variety of print and electronic formats and by print-on-demand. Some material included with standard print versions of this book may not be included in e-books or in print-on-demand. If this book refers to media such as a CD or DVD that is not included in the version you purchased, you may download this material at http://booksupport.wiley .com. For more information about Wiley products, visit www.wiley.com.

Library of Congress Cataloging-in-Publication Data:

Bulkowski, Thomas N., 1957-
    Trading basics : evolution of a trader / Thomas N. Bulkowski.
        pages cm. — (Wiley trading series)
    Includes bibliographical references and index.
    ISBN 978-1-118-46421-2 (cloth); ISBN 978-1-118-48831-7 (ebk);
    ISBN 978-1-118-48838-6 (ebk); ISBN 978-1-118-51694-2 (ebk)
    1. Portfolio management.   2. Investments.   I. Title.
    HG4529.5.B85 2013
    332.64—dc23

                                                    2012032671
Printed in the United States of America.

10 9 8 7 6 5 4 3 2 1

Contents

Preface

Are you like John?

He learned early in life to save his money for a rainy day. Instead of putting it into the bank, he put it into the stock market. He bought Cisco Systems in mid-1999 at 35 and watched the stock soar to 82 in less than a year.

"I'm looking for my first 10-bagger," he said, and held onto the stock.

In 2001, when the tech bubble burst, the Cisco balloon popped, too, and it plunged back to 35. He was at breakeven after seeing the stock more than double.

"It'll recover," he said. "It's a $200 stock. You'll see."

The stock tunneled through 35 then 30, then 20, and bottomed at 15, all in *one* month. When it hit 10, he sold it for a 70 percent loss.

"I should have sold at the top. Buy-and-hold doesn't work." But it did work. Cisco more than doubled, but he held too long.

Next, he tried position trading to better time the exit and chose Eastman Chemical. He bought it in 2003 at 14, just pennies from the bear market bottom, and rode it up to 21 before selling. He made 50 percent in a year. Was he happy?

"I sold too soon." The stock continued rising, hitting 30 in 2005. He disliked seeing profits mount after he sold, and wanted to profit from swings in both directions.

He switched to swing trading in 2005 and tried his old favorite: Cisco. The stock bounced from 17 to 20 to 17 to 22 over the next year, but he always bought too late and exited too early. He made money, but not enough.

He took a vacation from his day job and watched Applied Materials wave to him on the computer screen, inviting him to come day trade it. So he did. He made $400 in just 15 minutes. "If I can make $400 a day for a year, I'll make"—he grabbed his calculator and punched buttons—"$146,000! No, that's not right. How many trading days are there in a year?"

He redid the math and discovered that he could make $100,000 a year by nibbling off just 40 cents a share on 1,000 shares every trading day. "Wow. Count me in."

After paying $5,000 for a trading course and more for hardware, software, and data feeds, he took the plunge and started day trading full time.

It took a year to blow through his savings. Another three months took out his emergency fund. He moved back in with his parents while he looked for a real job.

Now, he is saving again and putting it to work in the market. "After reading the manuscript for this book," he said, "I found a trading style that works for me. I'm a swinger—a swing trader. And I'm making money, too." He handles not only his own money but his parents and siblings as well, providing them with extra income and building a nest egg for their retirement.

EVOLUTION OF A TRADER

John represents an amalgam of traders, a composite of those searching for a trading style that they can call their own. He suffered through many failed trades before finding a trading style that worked for him. I wrote the *Evolution of a Trader* series to help people like John.

Evolution of a Trader traces my journey from a buy-and-hold investor to position trader to swing trader to day trader as I searched for styles that worked best when markets evolved. However, these are not autobiographical. Rather, they are an exploration of what has worked, what is supposed to work but does not, and what may work in the future.

This series dissects the four trading styles and provides discoveries, trading tips, setups, and tactics to make each style a profitable endeavor. I have done the research so you do not have to. I show what is needed to make each style work.

CONTENT OVERVIEW

The three books in the *Evolution of a Trader* series provide numerous tips, trading ideas, and setups based on personal experience and that of others.

Easy to understand tests are used to confirm trading folklore and to illustrate ideas and setups, and yet the books are an entertaining read with an engaging style that appeals to the novice.

Each section has bullet items summarizing the importance of the findings. A checklist at chapter's end provides an easy-to-use summary of the contents and reference of where to find more information.

At the end of each book is a topic checklist and reference.

Trading Basics

The first book in the series begins with the basics, creating a solid foundation of terms and techniques. Although you may understand market basics, you will learn from this book.

How do I know? Take this quiz. If you have to guess at the answers, then you need to buy this book. If you get some of them wrong, then imagine what you are missing. Answers are at the end of the quiz.

From Chapter 2: Money Management

1. True or false: Trading a constant position size can have disastrous results.

2. True or false: A market order to cancel a buy can be denied if it is within two minutes of the Nasdaq's open.

3. True or false: Dollar cost averaging underperforms.

From Chapter 3: Do Stops Work?

1. True or false: Fibonacci retracements offer no advantage over any other number as a turning point.

2. True or false: A chandelier stop hangs off the high price.

3. True or false: Stops cut profit more than they limit risk.

From Chapter 4: Support and Resistance

1. True or false: Peaks with below average volume show more resistance.

2. True or false: Support gets stronger over time.

3. True or false: The middle of a tall candle is no more likely to show support or resistance than any other part.

From Chapter 5: 45 Tips Every Trader Should Know

1. True or false: Fibonacci extensions are no more accurate than any other tool for determining where price might reverse.

2a. True or false: Only bullish divergence (in the RSI indicator) works and only in a bull market.

2b. True or false: Bullish divergence (in the RSI indicator) fails to beat the market more often than it works.

3. True or false: Price drops faster than it rises.

From Chapter 6: Finding and Fixing What Is Wrong

1. True or false: The industry trend is more important than the market trend.

2. True or false: Holding a trade too long is worse than selling too early.

3. True or false: Sell in May and go away.

The answer to every statement is true.

Fundamental Analysis and Position Trading

This book explains and describes the test results of various fundamental factors such as book value, price-to-earnings ratio, and so on, to see how important they are to stock selection and performance.

The Fundamental Analysis Summary chapter provides tables of fundamental factors based on hold times of one, three, and five years that show which factor is most important to use for those anticipated hold times. The tables provide a handy reference for buy-and-hold investors or for other trading styles that wish to own a core portfolio of stocks based on fundamental analysis.

Chapters such as How to Double Your Money, Finding 10-Baggers, and Trading 10-Baggers put the fundamentals to work. The chapter titled Selling Buy-and-Hold helps solve the problem of when to sell long-term holdings.

Position Trading The second part of *Fundamental Analysis and Position Trading* explores position trading. It introduces market timing to help remove the risk of buying and holding a stock for years.

Have you heard the phrase, *Trade with the trend*? How often does a stock follow the market higher or lower? The section in Chapter 19 titled, "What is Market Influence on Stocks?" provides the answer.

This part of the book looks at how chart patterns can help with position trading. It discloses the 10 most important factors that make chart patterns work and then blends them into a scoring system. That system can help you become a more profitable position trader when using chart patterns.

Six actual trades are discussed to show how position trading works and when it does not. Consider them as roadmaps that warn when the road is bumpy and when the market police are patrolling.

Swing and Day Trading

The last book of the series covers swing and day trading. The first portion of the book highlights swing trading techniques, explains how to use chart patterns to swing trade, swing selling, event patterns (common stock offerings, trading Dutch auction tender offers, earnings releases, rating changes, and so on), and other trading setups.

It tears apart a new tool called the chart pattern indicator. The indicator is not a timing tool, but a sentiment indicator that is great at calling major market turns.

Day Trading Day trading reviews the basics including home office setup, cost of day trading, day trading chart patterns, and the opening range breakout. It discusses research into the major reversal times each day and what time of the day is most likely to set the day's high and low—valuable information to a day trader.

An entire chapter discusses the opening gap setup and why fading the gap is the best way to trade it. Another chapter discusses the opening range breakout setup and questions whether it works.

Ten horror stories from actual traders complete the series. They have been included to give you lasting nightmares.

INTENDED AUDIENCE

The three books in this series were written for people unfamiliar with the inner workings of the stock market, but will curl the toes of professionals, too.

Research is used to prove the ideas discussed, but is presented in an easy to understand and light-hearted manner. You will find the books to be as entertaining as they are informative and packed with moneymaking tips and ideas. Use the ideas presented here to hone your trading style and improve your success.

Whether you are a novice who has never purchased a stock but wants to, or a professional money manager who trades daily, these books are a necessary addition to any market enthusiast's bookshelf.

Acknowledgments

So many people are involved in bringing a manuscript to life, and I play a small role. To all of those workers at John Wiley & Sons, I say thanks for the help, especially to Evan Burton and Meg Freeborn. They ironed the wrinkles and made the trilogy presentable, even fashionable.

Trading
Basics

CHAPTER 1

How to Retire at 36

I was not born into a wealthy family with rich relatives who buy winning lottery tickets, nor did I invent website destinations that make billions when they go public, and yet I retired at 36. Here is how I did it.

The story began when I walked into a bank, hand-in-hand with my mom, and deposited my life's savings—just over $100—which was the minimum needed before they paid interest.

Each time the bank updated my passbook, I had a warm feeling of accomplishment. The more I saved, the more they paid me to save, and that reinforced a belief system that endures to this day.

I received a massive raise in my weekly allowance from 60 cents to $7.60 when my father started a new job managing a large apartment complex. I became a garbage man, moving hundreds of smelly garbage bags from the collection room inside the buildings to the street. I saved almost every penny I earned.

Five days after I turned 16, I got my first job washing dishes at the Gould Hotel. I spent more than two years there, earning $2.05 an hour. That was a nickel above minimum wage, so I felt fortunate.

When my parents moved away, I stayed behind and spent the last five months of high school living out of a hotel room. I worked part time washing dishes and doing odd jobs for the hotel until I graduated. I paid a token amount for room and board under the kind generosity of the owner, George Bantuvanis, and starved on the weekends when the kitchen was closed. The money I saved went to pay for college, but saving money is a theme that runs throughout my early years.

I worked my way through college by pumping gas or doing temp agency jobs, such as running the mailroom for the summer at a brewery. Too bad I dislike beer.

Within the first year of graduating from college with a bachelor of science degree in computer engineering, I paid off my $600 student loan, repaid with interest the $1,000 "startup" funds my parents loaned me, and was debt free.

My first professional job was as a hardware design engineer at Raytheon, working on the Patriot air defense system. I arrived early and charted my favorite stocks on a piece of graph paper hung on the office wall. While I used strict fundamental analysis for my stock picks, my officemate, Bob Kelly, closed his eyes, twirled his hand around, and plunged it into the *Wall Street Journal* to make his choices.

I tracked my selections, his random picks, and after six months discovered two things: (1) he was beating me, and (2) I did not have a clue what I was doing. I continued paper trading using price to earnings and price to sales ratios as my main selection themes. I pored through *Forbes* and *Fortune* in the company library and learned to love fundamental analysis. Value investing was king!

In late 1980, the prime rate climbed to 21.5 percent and in 1982, the stock market became an airplane taking off on a journey to the clouds. I participated by putting my savings to work in a money market fund and dabbling in no load mutual funds with my retirement savings.

Four years after beginning paper trading, I opened a brokerage account. I had no choice. The company where I then worked as a software engineer had a stock purchase program in which I participated. At the end of the year, they gave me a stock certificate, and the easiest way to sell it was through a brokerage account.

The first stock I picked was Essex Chemical. I chose that one because I liked the fundamentals and because they frequently issued dividends in the form of cash and stock. I made 88 percent on that one. I chose Nuclear Pharmacy next mainly because of its way-cool name, but also with an eye toward the fundamentals. I found the company buried in a prospectus of a mutual fund I owned. Since I already owned it through the mutual fund, there should have been no reason to buy more, but I did. The stock dropped and Syncor International gobbled it up on the cheap, handing me a 25 percent loss.

However, the next several trades did well, climbing 195 percent (Carter-Wallace), 123 percent (another run at Essex Chemical), and 56 percent (Rite Aid) before encountering a string of losses: –41 percent (Dynascan), –39 percent (Intelligent Systems), and –30 percent (Key Pharmaceuticals).

After about a decade of using fundamental analysis and value investing, I grew tired of seeing a stock double or triple and then drop in

Michaels Stores (Retail (Special Lines), NYSE, MIK)

FIGURE 1.1   The stock bought in 1990 for 88 cents was sold for $44.

half—or worse. I added technical analysis to prevent the large givebacks while still keeping my toe dipped in the fundamentals.

Then came my first big winner: Michaels Stores.

Figure 1.1 shows Michaels Stores on the weekly scale. Do not bother hunting for it in the grocery aisle. It no longer trades, and I will tell you why later.

The first buy, in March 1989, at a split-adjusted price of $1.28, happened just after it bottomed from a swift, one-day plunge of 26 percent in mid-February. Analysts call such plunges dead-cat bounces, and they will become routine for the stock (18 while I owned it). Price climbed in an accelerated fashion, spiking at point A. At the peak, I had doubled my money on paper (the high was $2.57).

Three weeks later came the announcement of a buyout of the company for (split-adjusted) $3.00 in cash and preferred stock in the acquirer. What I find unusual about the offer is the timing. It appears that the smart money was anticipating good news because of the run-up from the February 1989 low, especially the sharp move during the week ending at point A. Also unusual is what happened to price after the announcement: It eased lower.

Typically, when a buyout occurs, price jumps up, and then flat-lines like a dead animal until the transaction completes. Was this a case of buy on the rumor and sell on the news? Perhaps.

The deal collapsed in early December when the buyer could not find financing for the deal. Price gapped 14 percent lower and continued sinking in a quicksand of falling prices, eventually hitting bedrock in late January at a low of 88 cents. From the close before the deal collapsed, the decline measured a tasty 57 percent. Instead of doubling my money at the peak, I was looking at a 31 percent loss. Buy and hold turned into buy and bust.

That is when I had one of those eureka moments. I remember thinking that if the stock was good enough for Robert Bass and his Arcadia Partners (one of the groups involved in the buyout), then it was good enough for me. I bought the stock again and again and again (with *great* timing, I might add) and look what happened. In late 1990, price started moving up. By 1992, the gain from my lowest purchase price (88 cents) was 369 percent higher.

I still saved my pennies and invested them in other stocks with good results, so when the company where I worked decided to spin off/sell their manufacturing operations and the layoffs came, I was ready. I opened my wallet and started counting. If I spent no more than $10,000 annually, I would be flat broke at 65. Retiring and doing what I wanted sounded a lot more appealing than working for others, so I hung up my keyboard and retired at 36.

When I say *retired*, I mean I had no earned income for years. I started trading stocks more often, writing articles, and then writing books while leaving plenty of playtime. I still think of myself as retired because I can do whatever I want every day, and that is exactly what I do.

Anyway, back to Michaels Stores. Over the years, I bought it 25 times. In eight of those trades, I more than doubled my money with my best gain coming from the stock I bought in 1990 at 88 cents. When the company went private in 2007, I sold it to them at $44 for a rise of almost 5,000 percent. On those shares, for every dollar invested, I made $50.

When you look at all of my trades throughout the years, I at least doubled my money on 32 of them. When you couple that with a lifestyle that says avoid the name brands because the store brands are just as good at a fraction of the cost, it all adds up to one thing: retiring at 36.

CHAPTER CHECKLIST

If you need a checklist for how to retire young, here is how I did it.

☐ Work hard and save every penny you earn at a job that pays a good salary.

☐ Live as cheaply as you can and invest your savings with care.

☐ Find stocks in which a buyout collapses. Buy when they bottom.

☐ Hold those stocks for the long term (I held some of Michaels Stores for 18 years).

☐ Hope that they move up—a lot.

CHAPTER 2

Money Management

In movies you hear the phrase *Follow the money*, so money management is where our journey begins.

Are you like John? He daydreams of working two hours in the morning trading stocks and then catching some rays outside as he powers his bicycle over rolling hills or cruises around the lake in a rowboat, chasing geese. Instead, he is stuck working up to 12 hours a day at a dead-end job he once considered exciting. He opens his checkbook, looks at the balance, and then fires off an e-mail. "How much money do I need to start trading?"

That is a common question without a simple answer. Why? Because it depends on your circumstances. If Aunt LoadedMama left you millions, then you can probably scrape by. But if you are like me and do not have rich relatives or generous benefactors, then you have to depend on your own skills to feed the bank account. Acquiring that skill takes time.

Before going further, let us define terms.

- *Buy-and-hold investor*, or just *investor*, trades for the long term. *Long term* can be as short as six months for testing purposes, but it usually means years. An investor is looking for home runs, stocks that will double or more in price, often while collecting dividends from them.
- *Position trader* is similar to an investor, but tries to exit when the major price trend changes. Position trades often last months, perhaps up to a year, but rarely longer.
- *Swing trader* tries to catch the move in a stock from the start of a trend (swing low) to the end (swing high), or the reverse. The trades usually last for weeks to months, but not years.

- *Day trader* enters and exits each trade daily. The term is what people like John mean when they want to become a *trader*.

This chapter is about money management. It covers the basics, such as how much money you need to day trade, scaling in and out of positions, and leverage. I spice up the presentation with new findings and ideas that may touch your fancy, ideas that could make or save you big bucks as you build experience.

TRADING: HOW MUCH MONEY, HONEY?

I began as a stock market investor with enough cash to buy 100 shares of a $20 stock (about $2,000).

If John wants to invest and not trade, he can cut the buy price to $5 and start with just $500 (or less if he wants to buy fewer than a *round lot*—100 shares). That is all it takes to become an investor. Save another $500, and search for a second stock to add to a growing list of companies in a portfolio.

Eventually, enough stocks will populate the portfolio that it will be time to sell one stock and use the proceeds to buy another. That is called *turnover*. I discovered that when I had 10 to 12 stocks in my portfolio, one would be ready to harvest for a profit and a new one would be waiting for planting.

What if you want to trade full time like John? A $500 investment will not pay the fuel bill for several hours of flying your Cessna Citation. You will need more money. Let us talk numbers.

What is your cost of living? Mine is about $1,000 a month, excluding taxes, because I live cheap. Adding taxes, home mortgage or rent, car payments, retirement plan funding, emergency cash, and your breakeven cost could skyrocket to $2,500 a month, or $30,000 a year. And that is just to break even.

How much trading capital would a monthly habit of $2,500 require from the pockets of Mr. (or Mrs.) Market? There are about 252 trading days each year, which translates into 21 days per month. That means each trading day you will need to pull $120 out of the market. Easy, right? If you can make $200 a day then your annual income jumps to $50,400. Net $500 a day and your income hits $126,000. The taxman—and everyone else that wants a piece of your action—will send you a Christmas card!

How often has your current income doubled or quadrupled? Trading for a living is no different, so do not underestimate the difficulty.

Those income numbers power dreams, but please return to reality. In the following analysis, I used the PowerShares QQQs (QQQ), which track the Nasdaq 100 index, as the trading vehicle of choice. The exchange-traded fund (ETF) is a popular selection for day trading.

As of March 8, 2012, the Qs had a daily trading range of 35 cents. That is the median move from high to low each day for the past year. If you were a perfect trader and bought at the day's low and sold at the day's high (or the reverse), you could make 35 cents a share, on average. To make $120, you would need to trade 343 shares ($120 ÷ 0.35). With a closing price of $64.75, that means you would need $22,210 of trading capital to buy those shares, not including round trip commissions, exchange fees, data feed fees, and so on.

When I started practicing day trading, I was profitable only 48 percent of the time. Let us round that up to 50 percent and say that two days a week you make money, two days a week you lose money, and the last day you break even or decide not to trade. At the end of the week, you want to net $120 × 5 days or $600 (this assumes the month has 20 trading days).

On winning days, you have to earn more to make up for losing days. If we assume you set a stop loss order to limit losses to $120 before quitting for the day, the winning days would have to make $420 each to compensate ($420 + 420 + 0 − 120 − 120 = $600). That means you have to buy 1,200 ($420 ÷ $0.35) shares' worth of stock for $77,720. Ouch! Day trading is becoming costly.

All of this assumes you capture the full 35-cent trading range each day, which is impossible. You may be able to capture only 10 cents of that, raising the number of shares you need to buy to 4,200, worth a cool $271,950. However, you can make more than one trade each day; so as long as you can net $420 on your winning days and keep losses to $120, you can earn $30,000 ($600 per week × 50 weeks, not including 2 weeks for vacation).

Netting 10 cents a share per day is reasonable for day traders, but probably out of reach for beginners (they are lucky to break even). Trading once per day and netting a dime per share would require $300,000 in capital to net $30,000 annually. That $30k only pays for your living expenses, not trading expenses.

If you want to take a vacation, then you will have to boost the amount of capital used so you can afford plane tickets, hotels, and food to compensate for the two weeks you will be snorkeling in the Keys, chasing the lava flows in Hawaii, or chasing fish in a submarine like my brother did.

You have margin available as a day trader, so that could cut the amount of capital needed. You do not have to use margin, but it is available. You can make multiple trades on securities that have a high-low range wider than 35 cents, too, so maybe you can capture more than a dime per share.

Pattern day trading rules require at least $25,000 to day trade. I sat with one day trader who used a partnership and had to pony up only $5,000 to trade using 20 to 1 leverage (meaning he could buy $100,000 of stock with just $5,000); but the authorities are cracking down on such practices, and he had to find a new trading venue.

Used wisely, $50,000 in trading capital should cover your living expenses for a year with a bit left over for emergencies. Want to be able to buy new underwear? Then boost your trading capital. You can play with the numbers and cook the books however you want, but having twice the minimum $25,000 is a good rule of thumb. It gives you flexibility.

If you want to be a day trader, then have $50,000 available that you could lose. In all likelihood, you *will* lose it if you believe some sources I have read. If you want to be a swing trader, position trader, or buy-and-hold investor, then I recommend saving enough money to buy 100 shares of a $5 to $20 stock. As the portfolio value grows, use a portion of it to position, swing, or day trade. I took that route.

One study found that just 4 percent of traders make more than $50,000 a year. Do you really believe you can be one of them? Many say "Yes!" after studying the markets for a few months. That is like calling yourself a surgeon after spending $5,000 on a weekend course. "Sure, I can remove that brain tumor!" That is the easy part. The hard part is keeping the patient alive to make a full recovery.

- Investors can begin with a small amount of money ($500 to $2,000), but traders need more capital: $50,000.

ORDER TYPES: READ THE FINE PRINT!

Brokers have come up with all sorts of ways to say *buy* or *sell*. Listed are the more common order types, but check with your broker. I found out the hard way that the fine print could cost money.

- *Market order* means buy or sell *now!* When you buy *at the market*, your order fills at the lowest asking price that sellers are offering. When selling, the order fills at the highest bid price that buyers are willing to pay.

  Here is a trap I did not know about that cost me $840. I placed a market order to buy a stock three minutes *before the open* and then changed my mind. The order executed anyway! The stock dropped by $1.20 on 700 shares.

  The rule is this: The cancel can be denied if it is within two minutes of the Nasdaq's open (I missed the cutoff by six seconds). Check with your broker to see if it also applies to other exchanges and what the time limits are.

- *Limit order* sets a price at which to buy or sell shares. When buying, it means you will pay no more than the limit price. When selling, you will accept no less than the limit price.

- Use a *stop loss order* (or *sell stop order*) not only to limit losses, but also to capture profits. The stop loss order sells shares below the current *bid* price. When the bid drops to or below the activation price, the stop order changes into a market order and can fill at a price other than the stop price. Notice the order triggers on the *bid* price, not the last *traded* price.

- *Buy stop* was one of my favorite orders. I used it to buy a stock just above the breakout price from a chart pattern. To use the order, specify a price above the current price of the stock. When the *asking* price reaches the activation price, the order triggers and the stop order turns into a market order. It can fill at a price different from the stop price.

  Here is what the fine print says: When using a buy stop, the order triggers not on the last sale price, but on the offering (asking) price. That is exactly what happened to me on Hudson Highland Group (HHGP). I placed a buy stop a penny above a prior minor high, at 10.61, after the market closed and after reading their earnings report.

  The next day when I looked at the quotes, I found that the stock had dropped to 8.80, after opening at 8.83. When I logged into my broker to cancel the buy order, I found that my order had triggered at the high for the day, 10.75. On my chart, the stock never traded near or above the 10.61 area. My broker explained that the stock had a bid/ask spread of $2 after the first minute of the open and someone placed an asking price above my buy stop price. That triggered my order, setting a new high for the day even though no stock actually traded at that price before then. The price promptly returned to 8.80, leaving me with 15 percent loss.

- *Day order* and *Good till canceled (GTC)*. These are modifications on some of the above orders, setting time limits for the orders to execute. *Day order* means the limit or stop order is for the day only. GTC means it is good until canceled, but it usually expires automatically in a few months unless renewed.

- *Market on close (MOC) order.* The order executes as close as possible to the closing price, but there are time limits. Your order must be entered more than 20 minutes before the close (the idea being that it *will* be rejected if entered at, say, 10 minutes before the close). Attempting to cancel a MOC order within 20 minutes of the close *can* be rejected, too.

  Placing a MOC order after 3:01 p.m. *can* be rejected (the market closes at 4:00 p.m.). Your broker may have different time limits. In other words, if you want to receive the closing price, place a MOC order at least an hour before the close. If you want to gamble, ask your broker to place a MOC order no fewer than 20 minutes before the close. If he says *no*, then just sell it manually before the closing bell. Keep in mind that the last few minutes often see prices bounce around like balls on a pool table.

- *Conditional orders.* These are modifications of orders such as OTA where one order triggers another. For example, if you use a buy stop to purchase a stock then you may want to trigger a second order to set a sell stop on the purchase. OCA means one cancels another. If you only have $2,000 to spend on a stock, but have two buy candidates, you can use an OCA. Whichever buy order triggers first, it cancels the other so you buy only one stock instead of two. I use conditional orders to eliminate the problems described earlier.

POSITION SIZING: MY STORY

When I first started trading, I did not worry about position size because I did not have enough money to be concerned. I allocated $2,000 to each position and had few stocks in my portfolio.

Table 2.1 shows the average amount of each trade, based on actual trades. Over the years, I added to positions in the same stock, so a $2,000 per trade investment sometimes meant that I boosted the value of the holding to significantly more than just $2,000.

For 12 years, I traded stocks with a value of about $2,000 per trade, riding the bull market that began in 1982. I did own stocks before 1983, but they were from a stock purchase program at my employer, so I exclude them.

In 1995, I tripled the amount of money available for each trade to $6,000. If you look at the chart of the S&P 500 index on the log scale, 1995 is when the market started trending at a steeper slope. At the time, I had no idea what was coming, but increasing the bet size was a good call.

The $6k per trade lasted five years until I bumped it up to $10,000 in 2000. That was right as the bear market began (March 2000). Surprisingly, I did not cut the trade size to reduce risk.

TABLE 2.1 Position Size Over Time

Year	Average Amount	Duration (years)	Comments
1983	$2,000	12	Bull market begins in August 1982
1995	$6,000	5	Market trend increases
2000	$10,000	4	Bear market begins in March 2000
2004	$15,000	2	Bull market begins in October 2002
2006	$20,000	2	Bear market begins in October 2007
2008	$10,000	1	Bear market continues
2009	$5,000	1	Bull market begins in March 2009
2010	$13,500+	2+	Bull market continues

Four years later, I increased the trade size to $15,000 and then $20,000 after that. Placing trades at a *minimum* of $20,000 each made me nervous and with good reason. I write *minimum* because I calculated the share amounts so that I rounded up to the nearest 100 shares, making sure that I spent at least $20,000 per trade. Again, I purchased multiple positions in the same stock, especially utilities.

The 2007 to 2009 bear market began in October 2007. I sliced the trade size in half and then half again, to $5,000, waiting for the market to bottom. I remember cutting it once more to just $2,500 toward the end of that period, but the average remained at $5k.

Now that the bull market has resumed, trading at $2,500 or $5,000 levels is too small, but it has forced me to diversify among many stocks, building each position as the opportunity arises. Recently, with the bull market solidly in place, I have been increasing the position size while maintaining diversity.

• Adjust the amount spent on each trade according to market conditions.

POSITION SIZING BY MARKET CONDITION: BULL OR BEAR?

Table 2.1 illustrates an interesting idea, which is this: When a bear market begins, for every 10-percentage-point drop in the S&P 500 index, cut the position size in half. That way, as the general market searches for a bottom, you will still be buying stocks, but in smaller and smaller amounts.

The technique allows for increased diversity among holdings (small positions in many stocks, some bucking the bearish trend and rising) and a diminished chance of being seriously hurt (smaller amounts invested per position) on new positions. The idea is not to put $5,000 into *one* stock five times, but to buy five *different* stocks, each worth $5,000. Multiple positions in one stock should be the exception, not the rule.

Table 2.2 shows how this idea works. Suppose I have a portfolio valued at $200,000 and I want to own 10 stocks. I would allocate $20,000 for each of the 10 positions.

If the market dropped 20 percent from the bull market peak (entering a bear market, by definition), then I would cut the position size in half to $10,000. Instead of spending $20k for a new stock, I would spend only half that.

For each 10-percentage-point drop thereafter, I would cut the position size in half until it reached $2,500, which I consider a minimum.

Obviously, if you do not have $20,000 to spend on each trade, then slice off a decimal, to $2,000 (or use whatever numbers fit your budget),

TABLE 2.2 Position Size According to Market Index

Market Drop	Amount per Trade	Discussion
0% to 19%	$20,000	Do nothing. Drops of this magnitude are routine.
20% to 29%	$10,000	Bear market begins. Position size cut in half.
30% to 39%	$5,000	Position size cut in half.
40% to 99%	$2,500	Position size cut in half.

but follow the same sequence of cutting the position size in half as the bear market grinds down.

The 2007 to 2009 bear market taught me that this system works. In 2008, I lost 14.5 percent, but that does not come close to the shellacking the S&P 500 index took when it plummeted 38.5 percent.

As the market begins to recover, the bet size doubles. Thus, you spend more in a rising market and less in a falling market.

- After a bear market begins, cut the amount spent for new positions in half for each 10-percentage-point decline in the S&P 500 index measured from the bull market peak.

Once you have figured out how much to spend on each stock, size the position according to volatility. Here is a formula to do this:

$$\text{Shares} = \text{PositionValue} \times (\text{MarketVolatility} \div \text{StockVolatility}) \div \text{StockPrice}$$

PositionValue is the *Amount per Trade* from Table 2.2, adjusted for market conditions.

MarketVolatility is the daily high-low range (or ATR) taken over 22 trading days, averaged, and divided by the recent close.

StockVolatility is the daily high-low range taken over 22 trading days (about a calendar month), averaged, and divided by the recent close.

StockPrice is the most recent closing price.

- The position sizing formula adjusts for market and stock volatility as well as market conditions (bull or bear).

For example, say I have a $100,000 portfolio that I want to split into 10 positions of $10,000 each. Since the S&P 500 index is within a few points of its bull market high (less than 1 percent away), Table 2.2 says I can invest the full amount.

I decide to buy Gap stock (GPS) at the closing price of 21.19. Computing the difference between the high and low price each day, for 22 trading days, averaging the result, and dividing by the closing price gives a value of 0.0213. The same calculation on the S&P index gives 0.009.

Plugging the values into the formula gives: Shares = ($10,000 × (0.009 ÷ 0.0213)) ÷ 21.19, or 200 shares (I round up the result to the nearest 100). That would cost $4,238, leaving $5,762 to spend on the stock at another time.

After placing the trade, I would set a volatility stop (discussed in Chapter 3) below the purchase price. Let us assume that I bought it at 21.19, so I would send my broker a stop loss order at $20.15 or 5 percent below where I bought the stock.

- Size the amount to spend on each trade according to market conditions (Table 2.2).
- Adjust the amount spent for the stock and market volatility (use the formula).
- Use a volatility stop (or other method) to limit losses.

You can, of course, substitute the position sizing formula of your choice, but the idea of cutting the amount of each trade according to market conditions is worth considering.

Of course, this idea pertains to buying stocks, not what is held in a portfolio. If a bear market comes along, the value of a $200,000 portfolio is going to drop. The technique described above will help when you have an itch to buy as price drops. Buying stocks is often a mistake until the bear market ends. This method helps limit the damage.

HOW MANY STOCKS TO HOLD?

During the early years, the number of stocks I held varied, but numbered no more than a dozen. Often, it was just four or five. The number 10 is recommended often in literature as the optimum size for small investors. It is large enough for diversification and yet manageable. Mark Vakkur (September 1997) wrote that 85 percent diversification occurs by owning just seven or eight stocks.

That brings up two quick anecdotes. When I was working at Tandy, I visited the library downstairs in my off hours. I remember an older man commenting that he owned over 40 stocks and saying, "I can't keep track of them all." No kidding!

In the fitness center's locker room, another man said that he owned only one stock, placing all of his eggs in one basket by taking a huge position. "Just watch that basket," he said.

After the 2007 to 2009 bear market ended, I started buying stocks again. I plunked down $10,000 and bought a stock. Then I did the same with another stock and maybe added another $10k to the first stock. I am holding 25 stocks and one exchange traded fund, not counting another three mutual funds in my IRA.

In essence, I am running my own mutual fund, split into 14 industries (some are related, like eastern, central, and western utilities or various types of insurance companies). Almost all are positions I intend to hold for the long term, so trading is infrequent. That makes the large portfolio simple to manage. If I was actively trading, I would consider cutting the number of positions to about a dozen. Of that dozen, some would be core positions, buy-and-hold stocks like utilities owned for the dividends and long term gains, and one or two might be speculative plays with the remainder being those I traded.

I sold many of my stocks and moved into cash during the 2007 to 2009 bear market. However, I held onto core positions like utility stocks. When I started adding stocks, diversification became a problem. I owned large stakes in utility stocks such that something like 45 percent of my portfolio was in those. I trimmed the positions or sold them outright and used the cash to buy more promising stocks. Now, the largest position I own is just 7 percent of my portfolio, and it is an insurance company.

- Hold as many positions as you can comfortably manage while maintaining diversity.

A BETTER WAY? PORTFOLIO COMPOSITION

The preceding is what I used over the years, growing my portfolio in good times and downsizing the trade size during bad times. My style changed from buy-and-hold to position to swing to day and back again to buy-and-hold. Did I take the best approach? To answer that question, let us take a closer look at position sizing and money management.

How many stocks should you own? The answer depends on many factors (like age, wealth, investment objective) and your trading style. I show my recommendations in **Table 2.3**.

For people who **buy and hold** stocks, they trade their holdings infrequently, so the portfolio demands less attention. That means they can hold more securities in their portfolio. For diversification, start with at least eight positions, but that can grow to a dozen or two, maybe even more if you are comfortable holding that many.

If mutual fund managers can hold hundreds of stocks, then us mere mortals can manage 25. I think a good amount is 20, giving 5 percent stakes

TABLE 2.3 Portfolio Size by Trading Style

Trading Style	Number of Securities to Own
Buy-and-hold	As many as you can comfortably manage. That means 8 to dozens.
Position trader	Core portfolio plus up to a dozen position trades.
Swing trader	Core portfolio plus 6 to 12 stocks for swing trading.
Day trader	Core portfolio plus 2 stocks for day trading that do well when the market moves up and 2 that do best when the market drops.

in each security. That way, if any one issue suffers a collapse, it will not unduly harm the remainder of the portfolio. However, that also means that any screaming firework of a stock shooting to the heavens will not help the portfolio much, either.

When the number of stocks in a buy-and-hold portfolio grows above a dozen, then separate out the troublemakers. Focus on those. Not only are they in danger of dropping, but add to the list those that are nearing upward price targets. If you have a target of 35 for ABC Gum Company, for example, and the stock is at 33, then add it to your watch list. If GonnaDrop, Inc., looks as if it is in need of the paddles ("300 joules. Clear!"), then add it to the watch list, as well.

For **position traders**, I recommend having a core portfolio of stocks. These are buy-and-hold positions that you can ignore on a daily basis. Four to eight securities would work well, maybe up to a dozen. They represent stocks you see benefiting over the long term. You might own some utility stocks to collect dividends. Perhaps a precious metals exchange traded fund would be beneficial along with a sprinkling of mutual funds that specialize in international holdings. In other words, diversify the securities among different industries, locations, and types (individual stocks, ETFs, mutual funds, cash). For example, I own four utility stocks, two located in the central United States, one on the east coast and one on the west. That way, an earthquake, hurricane, or forest fire will not wipe out all four, I hope.

As a position trader, I found that when my portfolio grew to about 10 to 12 stocks, I began to get good rotation. I sold a security when it was time to do so and used the proceeds to buy a new position. I did not need to increase the number of securities held; I just rotated out of the weak ones.

Swing traders need to pay more attention to their portfolio than position traders or buy-and-hold investors. That means limiting the number of securities for swing trading. I found that I could handle up to a dozen securities easily enough.

For **day traders**, limit the number of stocks to two that do well when the market or stock is trending higher and another two that do well when the market/stock is falling. If you know those four stocks intimately, then day trading them becomes easier. You get a *feel* for how the stock behaves and that is powerful knowledge.

Base the *core portfolio* of day, swing, and position traders on the next higher level. I mean the core portfolio for a day trader can be composed of swing trades. For swing traders, the core portfolio can be populated by position trades. And so on.

- The number of positions in a portfolio can vary by trading style.
- Begin with a core portfolio of stocks, and add stocks to trade depending on the trading style selected.

HOLD TIME: HOW LONG IS LONG ENOUGH?

I read in a magazine that as holding time increases, the more likely it is that a trade makes money. Is that why day traders have such difficulty making money? I decided to look at the S&P 500 index from January 1950 to April 2010 and counted the number of overlapping periods in which the index closed higher from period to period. **Table 2.4** shows the results.

For example, over the 50+ years, the index closed higher 53 percent of the time on a day-to-day basis, excluding commissions, slippage, and other expenses. If you bought the index at the close of each day and held for a day, you would make a profit 53 percent of the time. If you bought at the end of each month and held for a month, you would make money 59 percent of the time.

Let us take another example to show how I computed the numbers. If you bought the index and held it for 10 years, you would have made money 92 percent of the time.

TABLE 2.4 Number of Times the S&P 500 Index Closed Higher

Period	Up Closes	Period	Up Closes
Daily	53%	7 Years	90%
Weekly	56%	8 Years	91%
Monthly	59%	9 Years	92%
1 Year	71%+	10 Years	92%
2 Years	79%	11 Years	95%
3 Years	83%	12 Years	99%
4 Years	84%	13 Years	99%
5 Years	83%	14 Years	100%
6 Years	86%	15 Years	100%

I used monthly overlapping closes in the analysis. By that, I mean if you bought in January, you would sell 10 years later, in December. Then I computed the February to January holding period with 10 years between them, and so on, each month beginning a new 10-year holding period. That is what I mean by *overlapping* periods. All of the rows in Table 2.4 have monthly overlapping periods except daily, which uses no overlapping periods, and weekly which uses weekly overlaps.

I found that for holding periods 14 years or longer, each period remained profitable. If you bought the index at the close of any month since 1950 and held it for 14 or more years, you would have made money. These results could change in the future, of course.

- The longer you hold a stock, the easier it is to make a profit.

HOLD TIME: MY TRADES

I looked at a frequency distribution of my own trades, for both winners and losers. Using the average percentage gain or loss over the annual hold time says that I made the most profit by holding at least two years, but less than four. During that time, I averaged 28 percent annually for hold times between two and three years and 36 percent annually for holding between three and four years. This tabulation does not include day trades, which would skew the results.

Conduct the same type of analysis for your trades and your markets.

- My best hold time is between three and four years long.

THE MONEY MANAGEMENT MATRIX

Peter Nilsson (December 2006) discussed the "Money Management Matrix." **Table 2.5** shows my version of the matrix. This is oriented not to the buy-and-hold crowd, but to the other types of traders. It does apply to the core portfolio and will help buy-and-holders time the market for better results.

Stock and market up: If the stock or market is making higher peaks and higher valleys, or if your favorite moving average (such as a 150 day/30 week moving average) is sloping up, then the stock/market is trending higher.

If you smile most days after looking at the value of your portfolio, or cannot wait to check how much money you made in the markets each day, then the trend is likely upward.

TABLE 2.5 Money Management Matrix for Long Positions

Trend	Market Up	Market Sideways	Market Down
Stock Up	Buy. Add to position if relative strength is positive.	Buy or hold.	Hold. No new positions. Watch for uptrend to reverse, bearish divergence and bearish failure swings. Sell a portion?
Stock Sideways	Hold. Look for uptrend to resume.	Hold.	Hold. Watch for downturn.
Stock Down	Hold, but sell if downtrend does not reverse. Check for bullish divergence and bullish failure swings.	Sell or sell a portion.	Sell immediately and remain in cash.

Stock and market sideways: A sideways trend means the stock is moving horizontally, with a moving average showing flat or nearly flat slope (shorter moving averages might look like the nasty edge of a hacksaw blade held horizontal).

Stock and market down: Down trends mean lower peaks and lower valleys and declining moving averages. If your hands curl into fists and your teeth clench after reviewing your portfolio most days, or if you lose interest in checking the stock market, then the trend is likely lower.

• Determine when to buy, sell, or hold by the stock and market trends.

The following discussion explores each of the three trends.

Stock Trending Up

If the **stock and market are trending higher**, then this is the time to be in the market with long positions. If the relative strength (a comparison of the stock to the S&P 500 index or your favorite market index) is trending upward, then add to an existing position because the stock is performing better than the market. If the relative strength line is dropping then do *not* add to an existing position; the stock is weaker than the market, so look for a more promising stock.

If the **market is trending sideways or down**, then be cautious because the stock's uptrend could reverse. A stock will follow the market 64 percent of the time (discussed in *Fundamental Analysis and Position Trading*, Chapter 19, in the section titled "What Is Market Influence on Stocks?"). If the market is dropping then consider taking partial profits on existing positions. If the **market trend is down,** then do *not* add new positions (because the stock will often follow the market lower). Check for bearish divergence with your favorite indicator (I use the Wilder relative strength index—RSI) and look for small M-shaped failure swings on the indicator chart (see Chapter 5 of this book, the section on Good Eggs: Indicator Failure Swings).

Stock Trending Sideways

When the stock is trending sideways, then that is the time to hold on and see what happens. Since the stock will often follow the market, watch how the market index is doing. Look for divergence on the Wilder relative strength index or other indicator on both the stock and the market index. That might give you a clue to the emerging trend.

Stock Trending Down

If the stock is trending down, then do not buy new positions and do not add to existing ones either. If the **market is also trending down,** then sell an existing position and remain in cash. If the **market is trending up,** but the stock is falling, the stock should reverse (remember, 64 percent of the time, it will) and follow the market unless there is something seriously wrong with the company. Do research to discover why the stock is trending lower. It will be helpful if the industry, to which the stock belongs, is also trending higher.

If the **market is moving sideways,** then it is probably a good time to sell unless you feel the stock is about to turn up. Check your favorite indicator for signs of bullish divergence or failure swings (in this case, a small W-shaped pattern on the indicator chart). Consider selling a portion of your holdings.

- Always trade with the trend. The general market, industry, and stock should all be trending the same way.

SHOULD YOU SCALE INTO POSITIONS?

Ted is a novice position trader who wants to know, "How much should I buy?" A buy-and-hold investor would take his cash and divide it into equal dollar amounts (buckets), spending each bucket on a stock. A $100,000 portfolio might contain 10 positions of about $10,000 each or 20 positions of $5,000 each.

Ted has his *core* portfolio setup the same way, but wants to concentrate his trading portfolio in just a few, large positions. His portfolio is valued at $200,000 with the first half dedicated to core positions, and the other $100,000 split into four positions of $25,000 each.

He plans to buy when price closes above the 40-week (200-day) simple moving average and sell when it closes below it. He decides to throw $25,000 into this trade, but does not want to spend it all until he knows the stock is performing. Therefore, he buys fixed share amounts (constant position size) as price rises by $1, until he spends the entire $25,000. **Table 2.6** shows the trades and **Figure 2.1** shows the position trade (A, B, C, D are the approximate buy points for trades 1 through 4).

As price rises, he accumulates more shares, 1,000 at a time, boosting the *current value* of the holding from $3,890 to $27,560 after Trade 3. Then there is a problem. He wants to buy more, but the cost, at $21,560 (Cumulative Cost row), is almost at his $25,000 spending limit. On Trade 4, he buys 430 shares, leaving a few bucks to pay for commissions, fees, and so on. He has spent almost $25,000 on securities now worth almost $35,000, for a $10,000 open profit.

The stock continues to climb, as Figure 2.1 shows, but he is out of bucks. He sits on the sidelines as price hits a high of 9.20, valuing the open profit at $15,800.

Then the stock begins to drop, but he is not worried. He trusts his system and waits for the crossover exit signal. It comes about 2.5 months later when price closes below the 40-week simple moving average. At the open the next trading day, he sells and receives a fill of $5.06.

The buy signal was at $3.89 and the sell signal was at $5.06, for a potential gain of 30 percent. How did Ted do? He lost $2,537! How can that be? Two trades were below the selling price, but three were not. Those three trades cost him dearly when he bought high and sold low.

- Trading a constant position size can have disastrous results.

TABLE 2.6 Money Management for Ted's Trade: Constant Position Size

	Buy	Trade 1	Trade 2	Trade 3	Trade 4	Sale
Price	$3.89	$4.89	$5.89	$6.89	$7.89	$5.06
Shares	1,000	1,000	1,000	1,000	430	4,430
Cost	$3,890	$4,890	$5,890	$6,890	$3,393	0
Cumulative Cost	$3,890	$8,780	$14,670	$21,560	$24,953	$24,953
Current Value	$3,890	$9,780	$17,670	$27,560	$34,953	$22,416
Open Profit	$0	$1,000	$3,000	$6,000	$10,000	($2,537)

Coldwater Creek Inc. (Apparel, CWTR)

FIGURE 2.1 A 40-Week Simple Moving Average Signals Trades (weekly chart).

Ted used fixed share amounts—1,000 at a time. Was that the problem? Let us answer that by seeing how Alice fared on the same trade, but using fixed dollar amounts. Her trades appear in **Table 2.7**.

Alice wants to make five buys of $5,000 each, so she divides the cost of the shares by $5,000 to get the number of shares to buy. Since she is using the Internet, buying odd lot amounts (shares *not* rounded to the nearest 100) is not a problem. She could just as easily have rounded down

TABLE 2.7 Money Management for Alice's Trade: Fixed Dollar Amounts

	Buy	Trade 1	Trade 2	Trade 3	Trade 4	Sale
Price	$3.89	$4.89	$5.89	$6.89	$7.89	$5.06
Shares	1,285	1,022	849	726	634	4,516
Cost	$5,000	$5,000	$5,000	$5,000	$5,000	0
Cumulative Cost	$5,000	$10,000	$15,000	$20,000	$25,000	$25,000
Value	$5,000	$11,285	$18,593	$26,750	$35,632	$22,852
Open Profit	$0	$1,285	$3,593	$6,750	$10,632	($2,148)

the shares, but I wanted to keep the two examples similar. At the end of Trade 4, her value is $35,600, but Ted's was $34,950. When the price drops on the sale date, her loss—and it is still a loss—is smaller: $2,148 compared to Ted's $2,537.

Just by changing the method of purchase, she has reduced her loss, so if anyone tells you that position sizing does not matter, tell them about Ted and Alice!

- Trading using fixed dollar amounts improves results, but not by much.

You might think that few use constant position size trades like Ted, but day traders often trade 1,000 share amounts. As the example shows, for other types of traders (swing, position, buy-and-hold), when multiple positions in the same security are anticipated, a constant dollar amount is better—at least in this example.

Pete has a different idea. He is a math whiz and wants to vary the number of shares purchased according to how volatile the stock is. He uses the following formula.

$$\text{Position size} = (\text{Portfolio value} \times \text{Risk}) \div \text{Volatility}$$

The portfolio value is the current value of the portfolio at the time of purchase. For the risk, he considered using 2 percent of portfolio value, but wanted a second opinion. He asked his friend Jacob, who has been trading since time began, what his historical loss was divided by his current portfolio value. Jacob had an average loss of $1,300 and a portfolio value of $390,000 for a risk assessment of 0.33 percent ($1300 \div 390,000$. This is an actual value from a trader). Pete decided to use the lower value (0.33 percent) in the formula.

Pete calculated the volatility of the stock using a 22-trading day (about a month) average of the daily high to low price swings in the stock. Some use

TABLE 2.8 Money Management for Pete's Trade: Volatility Based

	Buy	Trade 1	Trade 2	Sale
Price	$3.89	$4.89	$5.89	$5.06
Volatility	$0.245	$0.45	$0.435	N/A
Shares	2,694	1,486	1,231	5,411
Cost	$10,479	$7,269	$7,251	$0.00
Cumulative Cost	$10,479	$17,748	$24,998	$24,998
Value	$10,479	$20,442	$31,873	$27,381
Open Profit	$0	$2,694	$6,874	$2,383
Portfolio Value	$200,000	$202,694	$206,874	$202,383

the average true range (ATR), but he prefers the high-low value. **Table 2.8** shows his results.

On the day he bought, the stock had a 22-day average volatility of $0.245, meaning the average high to low swing in the stock was a quarter over the last 22 trading days. Plugging the numbers into the formula (Position size = (200,000 × 0.0033) ÷ 0.245) meant he should buy 2,694 shares, which he did.

On Trade 1, volatility almost doubled, cutting the number of shares purchased, but the portfolio value had increased by that time. On Trade 2, his program told him to buy more shares, but he had to limit them because he did not want to invest more than $25,000 in the position. Thus, he stopped buying the stock after Trade 2.

When the stock dropped to the sale price, only Trade 2 had a price higher than the sale price, so he made a profit of $2,383.

Have you noticed a trend here? The more shares bought at a lower price, the more profitable the trade. What if you spend the full $25,000 at the buy price and sell at $5.06? You would buy 6,426 shares for a profit of $7,518. Wow!

You might be thinking that we have discovered the path to riches! All we have to do is spend the full $25,000 on the first trade and then drive our 18-wheeler full of profits to the bank.

Not so fast.

Imagine that we buy the same stock at $3.89 but this time it drops $1 to $2.89 before we sell. The last method gives the worst performance. It loses $6,426! In other words, the best system has turned into the worst.

If the stock climbs, the more shares we own at a lower price, the better we will do. If the stock drops, the more shares we own, the worse we do. This is just common sense, but our examples prove it.

If the preceding is too simple for your tastes and you would like a challenge, then read Ralph Vince's book *The Handbook of Portfolio Mathematics*. It discusses optimal *f*, portfolio construction, and the leverage space model. After reading the manuscript, I thought highly of the work so my endorsement is on the jacket cover. Bring popcorn, and tell him that Tom sent you.

- Use a volatility-based position size for the best results in upward markets.

Testing Scaling In

Should you scale into a trade? That sounds like something from a horror flick, but it refers to buying a partial position instead of investing thy whole wad at once. To answer the question, I based the method on an article by Howard Bandy (October 2009).

The test period spanned from the first trading day in January 2004 and ended on the last trading day in October 2008. Over that period, the S&P 500 index climbed 41 percent, fell 42 percent, and ended 13 percent below where it began.

Test 1   Table 2.9 lists the tests, beginning with Test 1, the benchmark. The system used for all tests is a variation of the basic theme as follows. On the first trading day of the month, buy $10,000 worth of each stock (fractional shares allowed), and sell it on the last trading day of the month. Then start again the next month and continue buying and selling until the end of the test period. Do this for each of the 571 stocks in the database. Do not adjust for commissions, fees, slippage, and taxes, and idle cash does not earn interest.

Profits are not reinvested in the next trade. That means each trade buys $10,000 worth of stock. In Table 2.9, the **average per trade** is the difference between $10,000 and what remains at the end of each trade, averaged for all trades and all stocks in the test. **Wins** are the ratio of winning trades to all trades. The **small losses** column is a count of how often losses of 10 percent or less occur. The larger the percentage of small losses, the better.

Following this methodology, Test 1 wins 52 percent of the time with 74 percent of the losses smaller than 10 percent. The risk is $10,000, or the entire amount invested per trade.

The test does not scale in (add to an existing position) nor does it use stops. This is the buy-and-hold variation since it buys at the start of the month and sells at the end. It is the benchmark to which the other tests are compared.

Test 2   This test uses an initial 10 percent stop based on the closing price on the buy date, and then switching to a 10 percent trailing stop placed below the highest high as the trade progresses. If price drops to

TABLE 2.9   Scaling In Tests

Test	Average/ Trade	Wins	Small Losses
1: Benchmark, $10k invested.	$14.92	52%	74%
2: 10% trailing stop, $10k invested.	($12.43)	44%	98%
3: Scale in at 5% profit, $5k, 10% trailing stop.	($6.29)	39%	98%
4: Scale in at 10% profit, $5k, 10% trailing stop.	($6.81)	41%	98%
5: 10% trailing stop, scale in at 10% profit, $5k, raise stop to breakeven, then trail it higher.	($7.81)	42%	98%
6: Scale in at 5% loss, $5k, 10% trailing stop.	($0.95)	54%	92%

or below the stop price, it is sold at the stop price unless the stock gap opened lower that day (in which case, the lower of the stop or opening price is used).

The only difference between this test and the benchmark is the use of a trailing stop. Notice that when a stop is used, the system moves from a profit to a loss. Small losses (less than 10 percent) shoot up to 98 percent (which is good). The number of winning trades drops to 44 percent from 52 percent in Test 1.

The results suggest that you will make more money with buy-and-hold using this system, but if you need to sell, the loss could be substantial (almost $4k). Using a stop cuts the potential loss significantly, but you will not make any money because the stop cashes you out of winners prematurely.

- Using a trailing stop hurts profits but limits losses.

Test 3   Test 3 has cash set at $5,000 per position (two positions maximum per trade, for a total of $10,000) with a 10 percent trailing stop. Add the second $5k if the stock climbs 5 percent, based on the closing price. On the first position, the risk is $500, but grows to $1,000 after adding the second half. The stop is set such that the risk is no more than $1,000 per trade (except in those cases where the stock gaps open lower).

Table 2.9 shows that the average loss per trade improves to $6.29 from over $12 in Test 2 with 98 percent of the trades showing small losses. However, the percentage of winning trades drops to 39 percent.

The results suggest that scaling in increases profits even though the number of winning trades drops. However, the per-trade average loss does not come close to the benchmark's profit. Bandy's results using 72 high volume stocks and exchange-traded funds says that 65 percent of the securities did not rise far enough to trigger a scale in. I did not test that, but it is an interesting finding.

Test 4   This is the same as the prior test except that it scales in at a 10 percent profit, up from 5 percent. The test shows that the average loss per trade grew slightly to $6.81. The percentage of winners climbed slightly to 41 percent. Since the stock only has a month to climb 10 percent, few stocks (only 11 percent in Bandy's tests rise far enough to scale in) actually do that so the position is penalized for having only $5,000 invested instead of the full $10k.

Test 5   Begin with $5,000 and a 10 percent trailing stop. If the stock gains 10 percent then invest the second $5,000 and raise the stop to breakeven, trailing it upward at 10 percent below the highest high. Since the full $10,000 is invested, do not buy any more (in all tests, the maximum invested is $10,000, and sometimes less).

Risk begins at $500 and rises to $0. After setting the stop to breakeven, you would think that this test would show good performance. However, it does not when losses increase to $7.81 per trade, on average. The percentage of winning trades rises by one point to 42 percent. Bandy reports that this scenario is the worst performing of his tests.

- Raising a stop to breakeven is no guarantee of profitability.

Test 6   This test averages down, meaning it buys more if the stock drops. Begin with $5,000 (with no stop) and if the stock drops 5 percent (based on the closing price), buy another $5,000. After investing the full $10,000, use a trailing 10 percent stop.

Notice that the loss narrows considerably, to $0.95, but the losses over 10 percent grow (fewer are small losses). The number of winning trades climbs to 54 percent.

Bandy concludes by writing, "None of (the tests) demonstrates a compelling reason to scale into trades," and none of the tests beat buy and hold.

- Scaling in works, but only if the stock rises.

AVERAGING DOWN: THROWING AWAY MONEY OR SMART CHOICE?

I wanted to explore averaging down so I conducted additional tests that **Table 2.10** shows. Averaging down means buying more stock at a lower price to drop the average cost of the shares.

Test 1 is the benchmark discussed in Table 2.9 and is repeated here for reference.

Test 7   Divide the initial $10,000 into four lots of $2,500. Each time the stock drops 10 percent, buy another $2,500 until spending the full $10,000. No stop loss order was used.

As Table 2.10 shows, this test yielded a profit of $16.01, beating buy-and-hold. However, the number of small losses dropped to 91 percent. Just 2 percent of the trades invested the full $10,000, meaning most stocks did not suffer huge drops during the monthly test. Risk begins at $250 and increases by $250 until it hits $1,000. The number of winning trades increased to 56 percent.

TABLE 2.10 Averaging Down Tests

Test	Average/ Trade	Wins	Small Losses
1: Benchmark, $10k invested.	$14.92	52%	74%
7: Average down: Every 10% drop, add $2,500.	$16.01	56%	91%
8: On 5% drop, add $2,500.	$20.21	60%	91%
9: On 5% drop, add $2,500, trade every 2 months.	$32.08	64%	77%
10: On 5% drop, add $2,500, trade every 3 months.	$140.00	67%	72%
11: On 10% drop, add $2,500, trade every 2 months.	$25.81	60%	80%
12: On 10% drop, add $2,500, trade every 3 months.	$100.68	64%	75%
13: On 10% drop, add $2,500, trade every 6 months.	$335.71	69%	62%

Notice that this is the first test with profits that beat buy-and-hold. The results suggest that averaging down cuts risk and increases profits, at least in this test. Also notice that we are not adding the full $10,000 each time the stock drops. Rather, the test splits the $10,000 into equal lots of $2,500 and invests that.

Tests 8 to 10 Since drops of 10 percent in a stock over the course of a month seldom occur, I changed the prior test to average down if the stock drops 5 percent (Test 8). For Tests 9 and 10, I lengthened the hold time to 2 months (Test 9) and 3 months (Test 10), giving the stock more time to recover (or go down).

For Test 8, profits increased marginally, to $20.21 per trade as the number of winning trades increased to 60 percent.

The results for Tests 9 and 10 see average profits shooting up to the highest levels seen yet. The number of winning trades also hits record highs. The number of small losses drops from the 90s to 77 and 72 percent. That suggests larger losses take their toll.

By averaging in every 5 percent and holding for 3 months, the results show a near 10-times increase in profits.

Tests 11 to 13 The final three tests change the drop to 10 percent, but add additional time for the stock to recover: two, three, and six months for Tests 11 through 13, respectively. The average profit per trade rises from $26 to $336, and the percentage of wins increases to 69 percent, too. The number of small losses drops from 80 to 62 percent.

If you compare Test 9 with Test 11 (the difference between the two is averaging down at 5 or 10 percent), profits drop 20 percent, from $32 to $26.

The same trend appears for the 3-month hold time between 5 and 10 percent averaging down (Tests 10 and 12). Profits drop 28 percent (from $140 to $100.68).

Scaling In and Averaging Down Summary

With a gazillion tests, it can be difficult to figure out what is best. Let us review. The test period spans from January 2004 to October 2008. Keep the image of trudging up a long hill and jumping off a cliff in your mind because that is what the market did. Since the trades are mostly monthly based (in and out every month), many trades would make a profit if every stock behaved like the S&P index. However, the dozen losing trades at the end of the test period could wipe out any profits from the prior trades and end in a net loss.

Here, then, are my conclusions.

- Blindly placing stops will take you out of the most profitable trades, making performance worse than buy and hold.
- Scaling into a trade is fine until the stock drops. If that happens, the higher the buy-in price, the worse you will do. If you buy a stock, buy it as close to the optimum entry price as possible. The *optimum entry* is the breakout price if you are trading using a chart pattern, for example. You can also think of the optimum entry as your lowest buy price.
- Setting the stop at breakeven may make you feel safe, but it may not prevent losses. As Test 5 shows, performance worsened over most of the prior tests. According to Bandy, on a risk-adjusted basis, this test performed worst (of his seven tests).
- Averaging down works, but it depends on the hold time. **Table 2.11** explains what I mean.

TABLE 2.11 Averaging Down

Trading Style	Should You Average Down?
Buy-and-hold	Yes, but preferably only in a bull market or after an extended time (say waiting longer than 1.5 years) in a bear market (meaning, try to buy near the end of the bear market).
Position trader	Yes, providing you can hold the stock long enough for it to recover. Bull market only, and as long as the industry/sector is rising, too!
Swing trader	Not a good idea. If you expected the stock to turn and bought in too early, then average down only if the general market and industry/sector are rising. Only add to a position *once*. If you feel compelled to add again to a losing position, then sell it all. You made a mistake; trade like a professional and take the loss.
Day trader	No, because the stock could continue dropping throughout the day, leaving you with a massive loss when you have to sell at day's end. Your buying will not prop up a stock. A day trader I know lost *half* of his trading capital by averaging down. Do not do it.

SCALING OUT OF POSITIONS: A PROFITABLE MISTAKE?

Scaling out means selling part of a position to capture profits. A prominent day trader I know recommends selling the first trade of the day as soon as it shows a profit. Why? Because it sets a positive tone for the day. I think he is nuts.

After reviewing my trades, I learned that scaling out did not work for me. When I felt the need to sell, my instincts were right. Selling only part of the position often meant the stock would continue to decline, and I would sell the remainder at lower prices.

My scenario is different from the one the day trader described. His trade was moving up; mine was threatening to tumble. My question to him is this: If a trade is making money, why would you want to sell it? Just because it makes you *feel* good in a job where emotions should take second place is *not* a good reason to sell a winner. Selling winners and holding losers is the exact opposite of what traders are supposed to do.

Let us roll out tests to see what the numbers say about scaling out of positions. The following is based on another Howard Bandy article (September 2009).

Like the scaling in approach, I used 571 stocks from January 2004 to November 2008, buying each stock at the start of the month and holding it until either the end of the month or when sold by scaling out or being stopped out. I limited stock prices to a minimum of $2 a share because low priced stocks tend to move erratically, with penny changes meaning large percentage moves. No adjustments were made for commissions, fees, taxes, slippage, and so on.

Table 2.12 shows the tests and the results.

Test 1 The first test serves as the benchmark, the buy-and-hold scenario. The average per trade should be the same as the scale in test, since the test buys at the first trading day of the month and sells at the close of the last trading day of the month. However, this test eliminates stocks trading below $2 a share, reducing profits from $14.92 as reported in Table 2.9.

Winners occurred 52 percent of the time with small losses (losses below 10 percent) occurring 74 percent of the time.

Test 2 For all scaling out tests, I used a 21-day average of the high-low price change instead of the average true range or standard deviation to determine the scale-out price. At the start of each month, when the test bought a stock, I computed the scale out price. The scale out price is the difference between the day's high and low prices, starting with the

TABLE 2.12 Scaling Out Tests

Test	Average/ Trade	Wins	Small Losses
1: Benchmark, $10k invested.	$9.09	52%	74%
2: Scale out $5k.	$91.13	72%	73%
3: Scale out $5k, then set 10% trailing stop to breakeven.	$76.77	70%	78%
4: Scale out twice, $5k.	$69.46	72%	72%

day of entry and working backward for 20 trading days (21 days total). I took the average of the 21 numbers, multiplied it by 2, and added it to the closing price. The result is the price at which I would sell $5,000 worth of stock.

Why did I use high-low (HL) instead of average true range (ATR) or standard deviation? My testing of stop placement showed that the HL method sets a stop price closest to what I wanted with ATR and standard deviation coming in second and third, respectively. If the average true range or standard deviation is handier than calculating the high-low range, then use the appropriate one.

Selling half of the original position resulted in profits that were 10 times the buy-and-hold benchmark: $91.13 versus $9.09. Winning trades occurred 72 percent of the time and small losses remained numerous, at 73 percent.

Scaling out captured more profit than buy and hold.

Test 3 I used the same method as described in Test 2 to set the scale out price except after scaling out of the trade, I set a stop loss order at the breakeven price for the cost of the remaining shares, trailed upward 10 percent below the highest high. If the day's low price hit the stop or if price gapped open lower, the stock would be sold at the stop price or the opening price, whichever was lower.

Notice that the average profit per trade dropped from $91.13 to $76.66, simply because of adding a breakeven stop! Winning trades dropped to 70 percent (that is bad), and small losses increased to 78 percent (which is good).

Bandy, in his tests, found the same result. He wrote, ". . . Setting the maximum-loss stop to the breakeven price dramatically reduces profit." He used standard deviation to set his stop loss price on 72 of the most actively traded stocks and exchange traded funds.

Test 4 The final test shows what happens if you sell at a profit target. The test sets a scale out price at the time of the first buy and at the first scale out. The first scale out is for $5,000 and the second sells what remains. If either of the scale out trades does not occur, then the position is sold in the normal manner—on the last trading day of the month.

Profits drop to $69.46 with winners making up 72 percent of the trades, and 72 percent of them have losses below 10 percent.

A profit drop makes sense since the trade exits at a target price (the second scale out price) instead of waiting for the end of the month, when it could be higher (or lower). In essence, this method cuts profits (by scaling out) and lets losses run (when not rising enough to scale out). That is the exact opposite of how a trade should progress.

More Tests　The following tests separate trades into two categories, whether the stock closed higher or lower at month's end. The trade could have exited completely mid-month, but that did not matter for this category.

Table 2.13 shows the tests, and they are the same ones as before. For the buy-and-hold benchmark, the average when price closed higher at the end of the month over the start of the month was $694. When the stock closed lower, the trades showed an average loss of $766.

Tests 2 through 4 show that scaling out reduces profits. This makes sense since as price rises, fewer shares are owned, leaving fewer profits.

Test 2 begins to scale out of trades providing the stock rises enough to trigger a partial sale ($5,000 worth). In a down market, taking partial profits reduces losses, but does not eliminate them.

Test 3 sets a breakeven stop that trails below the high price after the first scaling out trade. This method reduces profits from the prior test, but also limits losses.

Test 4 allows two scaling out trades, the first sells $5,000, and the second sells what remains. The test showed slightly better results in upward trends, $411, but also larger losses, $510.

TABLE 2.13　Scaling Out Tests

Test	Up Trends	Down Trends	Change from Benchmark
1: Benchmark, $10k invested.	$694	($766)	None
2: Scale out $5k.	$452	($521)	−35%, −32%
3: Scale out $5k, then set 10% trailing stop to breakeven.	$405	($470)	−42%, −39%
4: Scale out twice, $5k each time.	$411	($510)	−41%, −33%

Look at the Change from Benchmark (far right) column. This measures the drop in profits and losses. For example, Test 2 shows a 35 percent reduction in profits over buy-and-hold, but the risk (loss) drops only 32 percent. In each test, profits shrink more than risk. In a perfect system, risk should drop faster than profits.

Scaling Out Summary

The results shown in Table 2.13 make intuitive sense. If a trade will become a winner, then the smart play is to hold onto the entire position. Do *not* scale out. If a trade will eventually become a loser, then sell the entire position immediately. Again, do *not* scale out of a trade. Even scaling out for a profit and then using a breakeven stop will not eliminate losses, but it will cut profits. Although I did not test this scenario, Bandy writes, "Placing a maximum-loss stop as soon as the trade is entered greatly reduces the profitability of the system."

If you are scaling out to reduce risk, recognize that profits will take a larger hit than risk.

- If price is rising, scaling out leaves money on the table. If price is dropping, scaling out means a larger loss than selling the entire position at once.

DOLLAR-COST-AVERAGING: GOOD OR BAD?

Grandma Moses dies and leaves you $12,000. Do you blow it all at once on stocks or spread the pain over a year? By spreading it out over a year, you buy more shares if the stock's price drops and buy fewer shares if the price rises. That method is called dollar-cost-averaging (DCA) and it has been around for a long time. But is it the smart play?

I programmed my computer to use the S&P 500 index starting from January 3, 1950, to May 13, 2010. At the first trading day of each month (February 1, 1950, would be the first buy date), the test bought at the closing price for that day and held it for a year (selling on the last trading day of the 12-month span—January 31, 1951), investing $12,000. Another test spent only $1,000 in February, but added another $1,000 each month until it spent the last dollar at the start of January. At the end of January, all shares were cashed out at the closing price.

I then repeated the test using the next yearly span, March 1950 to February 1951, in a series of overlapping, 12-month periods, until I ran out of data. I found that if you total the values from each yearly interval, the *invest it all, now* would have made $705,147. Investing a grand a month would have made $371,445. The *invest it all, now* group would have beat dollar cost averaging in 500 competitions (70 percent of the time), and DCA would have won 212 races.

In other words, invest the money as a lump sum. Do not invest it using dollar cost averaging unless you have no choice. By that, I mean it is appropriate if you are setting aside a portion of each paycheck for an IRA account.

- Dollar cost averaging underperforms.

USING LEVERAGE: AN EXPENSIVE LESSON!

Leverage gives you the ability to borrow money from your broker and invest it in the market, allowing you to go broke quicker. If you think I am kidding, let me tell you the true story of a trader I will call Nancy.

In the early days, she listened to friends and relied on trading journals, but only 40 percent of her trades made money, and several companies she owned went bankrupt. Then she started to do her own research and results improved.

Two years after entering the markets, the index dropped 56 percent in just over a year, bankrupting several more companies she held in her portfolio. She never thought of taking profits or cutting losses.

After losing heavily on one investment, she stopped trading for nine years. When she got back into the game, she switched from fundamental analysis to technical analysis, using pivot points and support and resistance. Her luck improved. In 50 trades, she lost only eight times (84 percent win/loss ratio), making an average gain of 60 percent per trade.

She entered currency contests sponsored by her broker, placed in the top five, and then made it to number one. Her confidence grew, and with the market trending higher, she made 2.3 times her money in just five weeks.

Then she switched to the currency market where 100-to-1 leverage is available—a mouthwatering amount. With one contract costing $1,000, she could control $100,000 worth of currencies.

If you have underage children in the room, shoo them away because here is where the story gets scary.

Until this time, the most she spent on any one trade was just over $5,000, and her largest loss was just $2,700. She went long 13 contracts of the British pound and U.S. dollar (GBP/USD), costing $13,000, almost triple her largest trade to date. Thirteen contracts controlled $1.3 million worth of currencies.

At the end of the first day, she had a paper profit of $6,600. The next day, the currency pair dropped, but she knew it would recover because her indicators said so, backed up by promising payroll data. At the close, she was down almost $19,000.

The next day, the currency pair dropped again, for a potential loss of $26,000—twice as much as her original investment. By the time she threw in the towel, she had lost $28,600 in just four days, *over 10 times* her next largest loss.

In one trade, she almost wiped out her account. If she had held on for less than two more months, her $13,000 trade would have lost a massive $110,000.

But that was not the end of her troubles. What followed was disbelief that the loss had occurred, anger at allowing such devastation to happen, and severe depression. How would she recover? How do you begin again when there is almost nothing left?

Welcome to the abuse of leverage. Ask any trader who has blown out his or her account if leverage was involved.

Here is another account from a trader whom I will call Fred. He writes, "I've been trading options only. I've lost 99 percent of my money since I began investing and trading and am down to my last $200. I started out in 2005 and until last year (2009) relied on dozens of newsletters which I tried one after the other—all lost me money and some of them cost a fortune just to subscribe plus the cost of expensive software."

Options are leveraged instruments because they control stock worth many times the cost of the option.

Options are great if you guess the direction, extent of a move, and time in which the move occurs. That is difficult to do even for experienced professionals. If you guess wrong on any of those three components and the option expires worthless, you lose your entire investment. Even selling a position before expiration can be costly, but many times, it is the smart thing to do.

I remember reading about one option trader who gets only a third of his trades right—but he makes money. Fred wins 42 to 43 percent of the time. Another option trader I asked said she wins 46 percent of the time. Of the three traders, only one is making money.

- Avoid using leverage unless you are a seasoned trader.

LEVERAGE GUIDELINES CHECKLIST

If the tales of massive losses has not persuaded you to avoid leverage, then let us discuss guidelines. If you have been trading the markets for less than five years, then forget about using leverage. You are too wet behind the ears for such a risky endeavor.

Look at your trading results. Count the number of trades that had losses of 25 percent or more over the past three years. I understand that sometimes huge losses occur, losses that are unavoidable, but leverage only makes them worse. If you have more than three (one a year), that is too many.

If you have more than three in the past year, then you are either very unlucky or do not know how to place stops. If you are going to use leverage, you need to place stops to limit losses. Nancy used a stop loss, which forced an exit, and she still blew out her account.

Look at the amount of loss you suffered on *every* trade over the past year and multiply each one by the leverage you plan to use. If you want to use only 10 to 1 leverage, then multiply each loss by 10. Total the losses and see how they would affect your account.

If none of this has persuaded you to limit use of leverage, then email me your story when you blow out your account. Your anecdote will be a cautionary tale for others.

Many of the horror stories in *Swing and Day Trading* describe traders zeroing their accounts using options or warrants. Try taking a different path and do not use leverage.

☐ Do not use leverage if you have less than five years of trading experience.

☐ If you have more than three losses of 25 percent or more within the past three years, then avoid using leverage.

☐ Multiply your historical losses by the amount of leverage you plan to use to see how the losses would affect your account.

CHAPTER CHECKLIST

In this chapter, we learned about money management, that it is a complex issue. I discussed how much money you should trade with, position sizing, constructing the portfolio, hold time, scaling in and out of positions, averaging up and down, dollar-cost averaging, and leverage—all of which tug on a wallet or purse when trading the markets.

Based on findings in this chapter, here are some tips to consider.

☐ The introduction defines the terms, buy-and-hold, investor, position trader, swing trader, and day trader.

☐ How much do you need to trade or invest? Answer: $2,000 to $50,000. See the section Trading: How Much Money, Honey?

☐ For definitions on order types, see Order Types: Read the Fine Print!

☐ Read the fine print on how your broker handles the various types of orders. See Order Types: Read the Fine Print!

☐ Adjust the amount spent on each trade according to market conditions. See Table 2.1.

☐ After a bear market begins, cut the amount spent for new positions in half for each 10-percentage-point decline in the S&P 500 index measured from the bull market peak. See Table 2.2.

☐ Size the amount to spend on each trade according to market conditions, adjust the amount spent for the stock's and market's volatility, and use a volatility stop to limit losses. See Position Sizing by Market Condition: Bull or Bear?

☐ The position sizing formula adjusts for market and stock volatility as well as market conditions (bull or bear). See Position Sizing by Market Condition: Bull or Bear?

☐ Hold as many positions as you can comfortably manage while maintaining diversity. See How Many Stocks to Hold?

☐ The number of positions in a portfolio can vary by trading style. See Table 2.3.

☐ Begin with a core portfolio of stocks and add stocks to trade depending on the trading style selected. See A Better Way? Portfolio Composition.

☐ How long should you hold a position to guarantee a profit? See Table 2.4.

☐ My best hold time is between three and four years long, but yours may vary. See Hold Time: My Trades.

☐ Determine when to buy, sell, or hold by the stock and market trends. See Table 2.5.

☐ Always trade with the trend. The general market, industry, and stock should all be trending the same way. See Stock Trending Down.

☐ Trading a constant position size can have disastrous results. See Table 2.6.

☐ Trading using fixed dollar amounts improves results, but not by much. See Table 2.7.

☐ A volatility-based position size gives the best results—for rising stock prices. See Table 2.8.

☐ Using a trailing stop hurts profits but limits losses. See Testing Scaling In, Test 2.

☐ Raising a stop to breakeven is no guarantee of profitability. See Test 5.

☐ Scaling into a trade works only if the stock continues to rise. See Test 6.

☐ The success of averaging down depends on the hold time. See Tables 2.8 and 2.10.

☐ For scaling in and averaging down conclusions, see Scaling In and Averaging Down Summary.

☐ For tips on averaging down according to trading style, see Table 2.11.

☐ Table 2.12 shows the results when scaling out of trades.

☐ If price is rising, scaling out leaves money on the table. If price is dropping, scaling out means a larger loss than selling the entire position at once. See Scaling Out Summary.

☐ Invest a lump sum at once. Dollar cost averaging underperforms. See Dollar-Cost-Averaging: Good or Bad?

☐ Avoid using leverage unless you are a seasoned trader. See Using Leverage: An Expensive Lesson! and Leverage Guidelines Checklist.

☐ See Leverage Guidelines Checklist for a checklist when thinking of using leverage.

CHAPTER 3

Do Stops Work?

I n the last chapter, we tested scaling in and out that used stops and made some preliminary conclusions about them. In this chapter, we take a closer look at stops, continuing to follow the money.

What is more important, making money or limiting losses? If you answer *both*, thinking that this is a trick question, you could be right. Both *are* important. If you do not make any money then what is the point of investing or trading the markets? If losses grow without bounds then your portfolio could be seriously hurt. Here is why.

Imagine that you have a portfolio worth $100,000 and you spend it all buying AToothpick.com because you heard from your best friend who talked to the janitor who no longer works there that the company has a new widget coming out. The stock climbs on the rumor and the value of your portfolio skyrockets to $150,000. On paper, you have made 50 percent!

A few months later, news comes out that their new widget was a flat metal toothpick that rusted not only in the box, but in your mouth as well, and sales are, well, flat. The stock drops 50 percent. That is the same move going down (50 percent) as it was going up, but your portfolio is now worth just $75,000. A portfolio that drops by 50 percent will take a 100 percent move to get back to breakeven. Based on this analysis, controlling losses is more important than making money.

Table 3.1 shows the numbers. If you suffer a 20 percent loss, it will take a 25 percent gain to make you whole. If you let the stock get away from you and suffer a coronary-inducing 75 percent loss, you will have to make a 300 percent gain—and that is just to break even! In other words, the smaller you can keep your losses, the better off you will be.

TABLE 3.1 Percentage Gain Needed to Recover from a Loss

Loss	Gain Needed
−5%	5%
−10%	11%
−15%	18%
−20%	25%
−25%	33%
−30%	43%
−40%	67%
−50%	100%
−60%	150%
−75%	300%

There are several ways to limit losses. One is to not trade or invest. Remaining in cash will not grow your assets much and inflation could take its toll. That is not a good option, is it?

Another way is to use stop loss orders. If you are a trader, stops can take the mental anguish out of pulling the trigger (buying or selling). Unfortunately, stops have a nasty habit of taking you out of big winners just before they explode upward.

- If you limit losses, profits will take care of themselves.

WHAT IS HOLD TIME LOSS?

Before buying a stock, traders and investors should ask, "Where do I put my stop?" That is a simple question with a complex answer. "Use a volatility stop" is my usual reply, and I will discuss the various types of stops in a moment.

Here is another way to answer the question. Research shows that using a stop hurts profits. The problem is that stops take you out of winning trades too early (which we saw in the last chapter). Thus, you need to know how far below the buy price to place a stop to keep you in winning trades.

I looked at all of my *winning* trades (excluding day trades). For the time I held the stock, I computed the maximum drop below the *buy price* for each trade. This is not the drawdown, which is the largest equity drop from peak to valley, but the largest potential loss during the life of the trade. I call it the *hold time loss*. **Table 3.2** shows a frequency distribution of the hold time loss.

For example, of those trades lasting less than a month, 57 percent of them had potential losses of 5 percent or less and 87 percent

TABLE 3.2 Hold Time Loss Frequency Distribution for Winning Trades

Loss	31 Days	32 Days to One Year*	Max
–5%	57%	16%	41%
–10%	30%	22%	25%
–15%	7%	11%	7%
–20%	5%	11%	6%
–25%	1%	11%	4%

* Few samples

(57 percent + 30 percent) of them dropped 10 percent or less. That makes sense because stocks often do not fall very far in short periods.

If you ignore the hold time, the right column in the table shows that 41 percent of all winning trades had potential losses averaging 5 percent or less, and 83 percent (the total of the Max column) of them showed losses of 25 percent or less.

The average hold time loss for all trades is 15 percent with a median of 7 percent. In other words, half the stocks dropped 7 percent below the purchase price sometime before I sold it for a profit. Thus, a stop placed closer than 7 percent below the buy price increases the risk of being stopped out.

That is a dangerous generalization because it really depends on the volatility of the stock. Nevertheless, if you have nothing else to go by, placing an initial stop 7 percent or even 15 percent below the buy price could allow the trade to fluctuate without taking you out of a winning trade and yet still offer some measure of risk control.

Placing a stop at 10 percent below the purchase price would protect me in 66 percent (41 percent + 25 percent) of the winning trades. If I set the stop at 10 percent, any losing trades would be limited to about 10 percent (there would be exceptions for stocks that gap open lower). Thus, a stop placed at 10 percent below the purchase price would limit losses while still keeping me in most of my winning trades.

You should perform the same type of analysis on your trades. You can add a profitability test, too, that will show how important those larger hold time losses are to profitability. In other words, if I used a 10 percent stop, 34 percent of my winning trades would be thrown away. How much money is involved in those 34 percent? If the biggest gains come from them, then I would want to increase my stop to allow more of them to succeed.

- The hold time loss can help you determine at what price to place an initial stop.

Let us discuss the various types of stops.

MENTAL STOP: FOR PROFESSIONALS ONLY!

A mental stop is one kept in your head instead of called into a broker. Seasoned day traders who focus on one open position at a time often use mental stops. They may not have time to place a stop loss order so they just watch the stock. When it is time to sell, they do so, and that is the rub.

Disaster begins when traders or investors try to emulate the pros. For example, Mary owns MBI Corp at $100 a share and has a mental stop at $90. The stock trends higher and reaches $103, so she pats herself on the back for making a paper profit. She knows the stock will not drop to $90, but if it does, she will sell. "They just announced a new widget."

She counts her paper profits and dreams of taking a vacation in Tahiti. "Imagine spending a week on the beach, with handsome waiters bringing tall, cool drinks with tiny umbrellas sticking out of them. Yum!"

The next day, she gets a quote on the stock and it is down to $87, off 14 percent from the prior close. Her mouth drops open. She searches the Internet for any news, and learns of an earnings pre-announcement that sales during the last quarter were weaker than expected.

Another large sell order pummels the stock. The professionals are selling, but she sits paralyzed as the stock pretends it is a skydiver in free-fall.

She scours the news and finds hopeful words from management that things will improve in coming quarters. She leans back in her chair, crosses her fingers, and mutters, "It will come back."

The stock, acting like her ex-boyfriend, is not listening. It drops to $85, a full 15 percent below her purchase price. "I have lost too much money to sell now," she says. She takes the picture of Tahiti off her bulletin board, crumples it up, and whips it at the wastebasket like a major league pitcher hurtling a fastball.

Three weeks go by before she gathers enough courage to get a quote. The stock rebounded to 93, but is at 79 now and rolling downhill like an 18-wheeler without brakes.

A week later, the stock is at 65.

When it hits 51, she decides to dump the dog.

The stock bottoms at 50 and then rises, making a V-shaped recovery.

A month later, it is back to 70. In another month, it is making new highs at 107, with no end in sight. Management is projecting a banner quarter.

The moral of the story is this: A mental stop is only as good as the mind that contains it. If you use a mental stop then you have to be able to sell when it is time.

- A mental stop is one kept in your head and not placed with a broker. Only seasoned traders should use mental stops.

MINOR HIGH OR LOW STOP: A GOOD CHOICE

Books about technical analysis often mention the phrases *minor high* and *minor low*, but what are they? I define them as short-term turning points in the stock. A minor high is the highest high of the five days surrounding the peak—five days before to five days after the peak. A minor low is similar except that it applies to valleys—a price lower than five days before to five days after the low.

I do not actually count the days surrounding each peak or valley to be sure it qualifies (unless it is during a test, in which case it is done automatically, and I often use two, three, or five days), rather, I visually qualify it. I am just looking for significant turning points.

Figure 3.1 shows minor highs at points C and D, and minor lows at A, B, and E. The AEB configuration is a head-and-shoulders bottom, in case you are

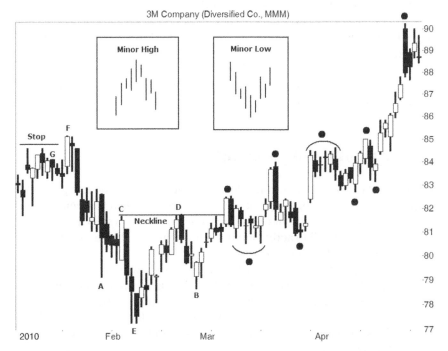

FIGURE 3.1 Minor highs and minor lows represent short-term turning points.

into chart patterns. Some of the minor highs (point C, for example), are not the highest peaks within five days since higher prices precede or follow. Not all minor highs or valleys are identified, and the black circles highlight other minor highs or lows. The two insets show the *ideal* type of turn you are looking for.

The reason I mention all of this is that minor highs and lows are favorite hiding places for stop loss orders. For example, if you identify the head-and-shoulders bottom and buy the stock, you might want to place a stop a few pennies below the right shoulder low (B).

If you shorted the stock at C, notice how price at D climbs to C and then turns down. Above C would be a good location for a stop—at least for a while.

Since everyone knows that traders place stops near minor highs and lows, market players sometimes try to force the stock to hit the stops (or at least it seems that way).

Consider Jennifer's trade in the stock. When price attempted to reach 85 twice, and then made a lower high and lower low, she shorted the stock at G and placed a stop loss order at the horizontal line.

Three days later, the smart money started buying like crazy, pushing up the price of the stock. It hit her stop, taking her out of the trade, and then what happened? The stock dropped. It did not just ease lower, rather, it cascaded down like water over a cliff. Not only was she hurt at being forced out of the trade, but the smart money rubbed salt into the wound by pushing the stock down, a tumble she expected, only she watched it from the sidelines.

- Traders know where others hide stops, and *magically* price tends to hit those stops before turning around.

SQUARING OFF ROUND NUMBERS

When using minor highs or minor lows as stop locations, do not place the stop right at the price of the peak or valley. Instead, add a few cents to the peak and subtract a few cents from the valley and place a stop there. In too many cases, price will exactly match a prior peak or valley and you do not want to be stopped out in that situation.

For example, if the peak is at 11.00, I will cover a short at 11.07. If the valley is at 20.00, I will place a stop at 19.93. I want to avoid round numbers (numbers ending in zero, especially double zero) since novice traders will place their buy or sell orders there. I want to be far enough away from those prices such that their orders give the stock every opportunity to turn before it hits my stop.

- Avoid placing stops at numbers ending in zero.

CHART PATTERN STOP: TOO COSTLY?

Chart patterns are nothing more than areas of congestion, often appearing as horizontal price movement. That movement forms patterns that tend to repeat. Each chart pattern has its own favorite location for a stop, but it is up to you to decide where to place the order. Place a stop below the congestion area in the belief that the chart pattern will support price in the future. If you short a stock, place the stop above the chart pattern since the congestion area may act as overhead resistance in the future. That overhead resistance will tend to impede upward price movement.

The head-and-shoulders bottom in Figure 3.1 is one example. Notice that the AEB pattern represents the turning point from down to up. A stop placed below the head (E) or right shoulder (B), would work well in this situation. You will want to raise the stop as price climbs, perhaps hiding it under minor lows. Notice how well that would work in this case.

One common problem with placing stops below chart patterns is the need for strong binoculars to see the stop. For example, if you bought at the neckline breakout (shown as a line connecting peaks C and D, extended to the right) of the head-and-shoulders bottom, a stop placed below the low of the pattern, E, means a drop from 81.77 (a penny above D is where I would place a buy stop) to 77.21 (below the head at 77.26), or almost 6 percent. In this case, that is a close stop, but many times the drop will be 15 or 20 percent, and sometimes more.

I built a web page detailing the best stop locations for most chart patterns: http://thepatternsite.com/Stoplocate.html. Refer to that for guidance on where to place a stop.

- Chart patterns represent good locations for stops because they often act as future support and resistance areas.
- Measure the distance from the stop to the buy price to make sure it is not too far away.

STOPPED BY A MOVING AVERAGE

A moving average is an average of numbers that is said to move as the most recent price quote is added and the oldest quote is dropped from the sequence. For example, if price has the following closing values, 10, 11, 12, and 13, the average is $(10 + 11 + 12 + 13) \div 4$ or 11.50. Four is a count of the number of price quotes used. If we averaged five numbers then we would divide the total by five instead of four.

Say another closing price comes in and it is 14. The moving average would be $(11 + 12 + 13 + 14) \div 4$ or 12.50. We drop 10 since it is the oldest and add 14, dividing by four. This would represent a 4-day or 4-period simple moving average.

If you were to plot the moving average on a chart, it would hug price as it waves up and down. The higher the number of days used in a moving average calculation, such as a 200-day moving average, the flatter the line appears and the more lag (delay) is introduced. Lag means it takes longer for changes in price to reflect in the moving average. Short moving averages look choppy and hug price closer with little lag.

Stan Weinstein recommends using a 30-week simple moving average for long term investing. I discuss his implementation in detail under in the "Using Trailing Stops to Sell" section in *Fundamental Analysis and Position Trading*, Chapter 16. Briefly, when price makes a minor low *and then recovers*, place a stop directly below the *date* of the minor low at a price slightly below the moving average.

The coming section titled, Trendline Stop, shows an example of how to do this with a trendline instead of a moving average. The procedure is the same, just pretend the trendline is a moving average.

- When price rises to a new high, place a stop directly below the prior minor low and below the moving average at that minor low.

THE TRUTH ABOUT TRENDLINES

Since we have already mentioned trendlines, let us take a moment to discuss them. Draw up-sloping trendlines along valleys and down-sloping trendlines along peaks. The idea is to line up price so that it touches, but does not pierce the trendline, multiple times. When price *does* pierce the trendline, it is one indication of a trend change. It does *not* mean that the trend has changed from up to down or down to up, but it is a clue.

Figure 3.2 shows an example of trendline AB extended into the future. Price touches the trendline multiple times as it travels from A to B. A well-constructed trendline should have at least three touches, but just two will do in a pinch. As price develops, it touches the trendline at G but pierces it at H.

Notice that after price pierces the trendline at L, it bottoms and then begins trending again. It follows another trendline higher, MN, before piercing this one and dropping like granite through water.

I tested trendlines for my book, *Trading Classic Chart Patterns* (Wiley, 2002), so refer to that book for proof on what I list below. When I write, "outperform," that is a measure of the price drop or rise *after the trendline ends*.

FIGURE 3.2 Trendline stops (circles) follow the stock higher.

- Draw up-sloping trendlines along valleys; down-sloping trendlines along peaks.
- Trendlines with wide touch spacing (averaging 29 days between touches) outperform those with narrow spacing.
- Trendlines with more touches outperform.
- Longer trendlines outperform shorter ones.
- The steeper the trendline angle, the worse the performance (price does not drop as far after penetration of a steep trendline, for example).
- When volume follows the direction of the trendline (up for up-sloping trendlines and down for down-sloping trendlines), the trendline outperforms.

TRENDLINE STOP

A trendline stop is like a moving average stop without the work of calculating a moving average. When price advances to a new high, place a stop slightly below the prior minor low and below the trendline. Raise the stop as price climbs and new minor lows appear.

Figure 3.2 shows an example of how a trendline stop works. The inset shows the ideal case of price moving up following a trendline higher. Price peaks at C, drops to E, and then bounces off the trendline on its way to D. When price approaches D, which is near C's price level, place a stop a few cents below the trendline at minor low E. That is almost all there is to trendline stops.

After taking a licking on MBI, Mary switches to Crane, shown in the figure. She sees the head-and-shoulders bottom with a left shoulder (LS), head, and right shoulder (A) form, but does not take action until price closes above the neckline.

The neckline is a line drawn connecting the two armpits of the head-and-shoulders (O and P), but, in this case, the neckline slopes upward so she just uses the high of the right armpit as the buy price (shown by horizontal line Q). When price gaps open, she buys and receives a fill at the opening price of 25.15. She places her first stop below the prior minor low, at B, at 22.91 (below round number 23.00).

She draws trendline AB and extends it into the future. When price approaches F, she raises her stop to below the trendline at G. When price climbs to I, she raises her stop below the trendline, at H.

She continues raising the stop in a similar manner until she sees the tight congestion region at J. This is where she changes tactics. Mary believes that a downward breakout from this region is going to take price lower, perhaps to her stop at K, so she decides to tighten the stop. She moves the stop to a penny below the congestion region and receives a fill at 32.47. On the trade, she makes almost 30 percent.

- Use a trendline for stop placement. Trail a stop upward as price rises, beneath a trendline at the prior minor low. Tighten the stop if price moves sideways, forming a congestion region.

FIBONACCI RETRACE STOP: DEAL OR DUD?

Most of you probably know about the Fibonacci number sequence, how it came about, how to calculate it, and how nature makes use of it. If not, then that is too bad because I am not going to discuss any of that either. The book, *Candlesticks, Fibonacci, and Chart Pattern Trading Tools* (Wiley 2003), by Robert Fischer and Jens Fischer, gives an entertaining introduction to the subject.

The idea behind a Fib retrace stop is that price will turn after retracing 38, 50, or 62 percent of the prior rise. This type of stop comes in handy during a long straight-line run when the closest minor low would be too far away to park a stop underneath. Although I refer to the percentages as Fibonacci numbers, they are mathematical derivations from the Fibonacci number sequence.

Figure 3.3 shows several examples. Let us discuss the ABC move (I chose the BC decline because it is proportional to the AB rise). Point A has a low of 43.10 and B has a high of 55.48, for a height of 12.38 (55.48 – 43.10). Applying the 38, 50, and 62 percent retrace values, we get 50.78, 49.29, and 47.80, respectively, which are shown on the chart. The first value, 50.78, is found by taking 38 percent of the 12.38 height to get 4.70, which is then subtracted from the high price: 55.48 – (12.38 × 38 percent) = 50.78. The same logic applies to the 50 and 62 percent retrace values.

Move AD retraces 50 percent before moving higher. The move from E to F retraces 62 percent (to G) before attempting a new high. The EF climb is a straight-line run where the Fib retrace applies best. A stop below minor low E works until price climbs too far (meaning a stop would give back too much money).

After computing a stop price, place it *below* the result since price will often drop to the retrace value before rebounding. In these types of situations, I always assume price will turn at the 62 percent retrace value,

FIGURE 3.3 A Fibonacci stop below C would work well.

so that is the one I use (meaning I do not use the 38 and 50 percent values). If price drops below 62 percent, then I consider that the market is telling me it is going down and either sell the position immediately or let the stop exit the position.

- A Fibonacci stop is useful for straight-line runs where the prior minor low might be too far away from the current price. Set a stop below the 62 percent (or 67 percent, see below) retrace value.

Fibonacci Tests Contradiction

I conducted two tests of Fibonacci retraces. The first used 766 stocks from 1994 to mid-2006, finding 1,956 samples with 525 of them coming from inverted and ascending scallop chart patterns and the rest found manually (as were the scallop patterns).

I looked at the relationship between rise and retrace, and discovered that the most frequent percentage retraces were 61, 56, 50, 55, and 44/59 (tie), respectively. The 61 percent number is close to the 61.8 percent Fibonacci retrace value, and 50 percent is dead on.

The median retrace was 59 percent, and a third of the samples stopped declining before reaching a 50 percent retrace. I concluded that a stop placed at a 67 percent retrace (yes, 67 percent) of the prior up move would protect a position from being stopped out 66 percent of the time. For more details about the study, visit http://thepatternsite.com/fib.html.

- Place a stop a penny or two below the 67 percent retrace of the prior move up.

Another test concluded that Fibonacci numbers were no more effective than any other number. For this test, I programmed my computer to find all minor highs above any peak within five days (before and after) and lows below any valley within five days (before and after). I measured the rise from valley to peak and the resulting retrace from peak to valley. I found 23,921 samples in 576 stocks from January 1995 to October 2009, but not all stocks covered the entire period.

This more extensive test created a curve of results that resembled a bell shape with no spikes at 38, 50, or 62 percent as one would expect to see. I concluded that using Fibonacci retracements offers no advantage over using any other number as a turning point. You can find the full study here: http://thepatternsite.com/SwingSetup.html.

- Fibonacci retracements offer no advantage over any other number as a turning point.

FIXED PERCENTAGE TRAILING STOP

Did your mom ever slap your hand, wave her finger in front of your face, and say, "*Always* use a stop!" Mine didn't either, but if she had, she might have been talking about a fixed percentage stop.

They work like the following: After buying a stock, place a stop 8, 10 percent, or any other percentage below the buy price. For example, if you receive a fill at $10, then a 10 percent stop would go at $8.93 ($9.00 stop, but placed a few pennies below the round number).

When price climbs, trail the stop upward. What does that mean? If the stock climbs to $30, a stop remaining at $8.93 is too far away to be of much use. Raise the stop as price makes a new high. If the stock rises to $11, place a 10 percent stop at 9.87 (a few pennies below the round number 9.90).

When setting the stop, what percentage should you use? That is the problem with this stop type. If the stock is volatile, normal price fluctuations will hit a stop placed too close, potentially cashing you out of a big winner. That could feel like giving away a lottery ticket as a birthday present and then finding out that it won. The solution to the percentage problem is to use a volatility stop.

- A fixed percentage trailing stop uses a constant percentage below the *high water mark* as a stop price.

VOLATILITY STOP

Mark is a novice trader who wants to make money, lots of money, but he does not want to lose a penny. He places a stop on every trade, but placed just 1 or 2 percent below his buy price. Within a day or two, he gets stopped out, taking small losses. Rarely, though, the stock climbs immediately and makes him a few bucks before the too-close trailing stop takes him out.

"Can you help me, Tom?" he asked. "What am I doing wrong?"

I told him that his tight stops were making him broker and his broker richer. I tried all sorts of explanations to convince him to use a wider stop, but nothing I said worked. He is an example of where the mental aspects of trading crippled his performance.

What he should have used is a volatility stop. I learned about it from Perry Kaufman (Wiley, 2003). A volatility stop is a trailing stop that is based on how volatile a stock is. Often, volatility is based on the true range, standard deviation, or high-low range of the stock. My tests revealed that the high-low range worked best followed by true range and standard deviation, respectively. Use whichever method is most convenient for you.

To compute a volatility stop, find the difference between the high and low prices each day for 22 days and take the average, multiply it by 2, and subtract it from the current *low*. The result is the stop price. Testing on actual trades found that 22 days and a 2 multiplier worked best, but different test methods and your trades may give different results.

Table 3.3 shows an example of the volatility stop calculation for Boeing shown in Figure 3.3.

The average difference of the high-low price range each day is $2.33. Multiplied by 2 gives 4.66. With the current low at 67.30, the stop should be placed no closer than 67.30 − 4.66 or $62.64.

You can substitute the average true range (ATR) or standard deviation instead of the high-low average since many software packages have those tools built in.

- A volatility stop helps prevent a position from being stopped out on normal price fluctuations.

TABLE 3.3 Volatility Stop Calculation for Boeing

Date	High	Low	Diff
04/19/2010	71.28	70.16	1.12
04/20/2010	71.98	70.95	1.03
04/21/2010	74.65	71.51	3.14
04/22/2010	76.00	73.68	2.32
04/23/2010	75.68	74.55	1.13
04/26/2010	75.29	74.14	1.15
04/27/2010	74.93	72.23	2.70
04/28/2010	72.99	71.34	1.65
04/29/2010	74.00	72.67	1.33
04/30/2010	74.48	72.26	2.22
05/03/2010	74.70	72.46	2.24
05/04/2010	73.45	72.23	1.22
05/05/2010	72.04	70.44	1.60
05/06/2010	71.49	62.00	9.49
05/07/2010	69.12	65.80	3.32
05/10/2010	71.73	69.80	1.93
05/11/2010	72.67	70.14	2.53
05/12/2010	73.37	72.04	1.33
05/13/2010	73.30	71.56	1.74
05/14/2010	71.40	68.98	2.42
05/17/2010	70.37	67.62	2.75
05/18/2010	70.13	67.30	2.83
Average			2.33

CHANDELIER STOP LEAVES YOU HANGING

The chandelier stop is a variation of a volatility stop and vice versa. It *hangs* the stop off the highest daily high price. The multiplier typically varies from 2 to 5, and the average true range covers up to about a month (21 trading days). In testing, I used a 3 multiplier and 21 days for the ATR.

For Boeing data in Table 3.3 (for convenience, I am using the same volatility reading of 2.33), the stop would be 70.13 − (3 × 2.33) or 63.14. That is a bit closer to the stock than the 62.64 volatility stop.

The next section tests the various stop types.

- A chandelier stop hangs off the high price.

TESTING SIX STOP TYPES

To test the various types of stops, I used 570 stocks from March 20, 2000, to July 9, 2007, yielding sample counts (trades) that ranged from 16,150 to 24,625. Not all stocks covered the entire period. The S&P 500 over that period made a long V-shaped bottom, beginning and ending near the same price. If you were to buy and hold throughout the period, you would have nothing to show for the risk. The stocks used are those that I follow on a daily basis and they range from small to large cap, low to high price.

I used a simple moving average crossover scheme as the method to test stops. Here are the rules.

- Buy when the closing price crosses from below to above the 50-day simple moving average of daily *high* prices. Buy at the opening price the day after the signal.
- Sell when the closing price crosses from above to below the 50-day simple moving average of daily *low* prices. Sell at the opening price the day after the signal.
- Exclude trades with closing prices below $1 at purchase time.
- Buy $10,000 worth of shares for each trade.
- If a stop is used, trail the stop upward, never lowering the stop price. If price hits the stop, the trade exits at the lower of the stop price or the day's opening price. For example, if the stock gaps open below the stop price, the sell order fills at the opening price and not the stop price.
- Commissions, slippage, and other fees were not included.

The use of daily high and low prices helps prevent whipsaws, that of a trade ending a few days after entry when price reverses. I excluded any buy signal if the stock was priced on or below $1 because low priced stocks are too volatile and the number of shares involved can be unrealistically high. A 50-cent stock that gains or drops a nickel changes by 10 percent and you would be buying 20,000 shares. If a stock dropped below $1 after buying, that is fine. I bought approximately $10,000 worth of shares, rounded to the nearest share. All stops are trailing stops, meaning I moved them higher as price climbed and never lowered them.

Table 3.4 shows the results, sorted by **Profit/Loss,** which is the average of sales proceeds minus the cost of shares. This includes both profits and losses. The **Avg Loss** column is the average loss for *losing trades only.* I consider this the risk column.

Hold Time is the average time owning the stock in calendar days. **Stopped Out** is how often a stop forced an exit from the trade instead of the moving average crossover rule. The **Win/Loss** column is a percentage of how often a profitable trade occurred. The **Profit/Risk Change** column shows the percentage change in profit and risk compared to buy and hold. A stop should limit risk more than it limits profit, so profit falling (a low percentage drop) smaller than risk (a high percentage drop) is preferable.

Results Summary

Notice that not using stops (buy and hold) gives the highest average profit: $232. As soon as stops are used, profitability suffers dramatically. That agrees with results of tests discussed earlier.

The average loss for losing trades remains small—about 5 percent ($500 ÷ $10,000 per trade). Hold time hovers around a month or so.

TABLE 3.4 Results of Various Stop Tests, Sorted by Profit per Trade

Test Type	Profit/ Loss	Avg Loss	Hold Time	Stopped Out	Win/ Loss	Profit/Risk Change
Buy & Hold– Benchmark	$232	($562)	47 days	0%	33%	0%/0%
Minor Low	$106	($436)	25 days	73%	34%	−54%/−22%
10% Fixed Percentage	$91	($500)	33 days	47%	34%	−61%/−11%
ATR	$79	($487)	26 days	68%	36%	−66%/−13%
8% Fixed Percentage	$77	($455)	28 days	61%	35%	−67%/−19%
Volatility	$76	($476)	24 days	71%	36%	−67%/−15%
Chandelier	$70	($486)	25 days	67%	36%	−70%/−14%
5% Fixed Percentage	$35	($349)	16 days	85%	36%	−85%/−38%
Top stop exit only	$124	($689)	26 days	100%	55%	−47%/+23%
Top stop with MA exit	$88	($540)	20 days	47%	44%	−62%/−4%

The win/loss ratio is about 35 percent, meaning two-thirds of the trades lose money, but the system is profitable overall. When compared to buy and hold, stops limit profit substantially more than they limit risk.

- Stops cut profit more than they limit risk.

The following discusses each stop test.

Buy and Hold The buy-and-hold test buys and sells using the crossover scheme with no stops used. It results in the highest average profit per trade, but also the most risk (Average Loss). Trades make an average of $232 each, but suffer losses of $562 along the way, and only a third of the trades show a profit.

Minor Low I programmed my computer to find all minor lows in the test period. For this test, a minor low is a valley lower than three days before to three days after the low (seven days total). The idea is that a trader buying a stock will place a stop a penny below the most recent minor low, and that is what the computer used, too. I removed trades with a minor low stop above the buy price and within three days of the buy date from being used. Why? Because a minor low three days away or closer would effectively look into the future. That is cheating.

Tests show that profits were second only to the benchmark, and risk dropped, too.

My guess as to why this stop method worked better than the others is that the minor low could be considerably below where price is trading, allowing the stock more room to fluctuate before hitting the stop. Notice that profit dropped 54 percent, but risk only dropped 22 percent when using the stop. That trend applies to all of the stops.

5 Percent, 8 Percent, 10 Percent Fixed Percentage These tests set an initial stop 5, 8, or 10 percent below the buy price and trail it upward by the same amount (5, 8, and 10 percent, respectively) below the current close. The stop is never lowered.

The higher the fixed percentage, the more profits accumulate and the higher the risk. For example, the 10 percent rate makes more than the 8 percent rate, and the 8 percent rate earns more than the 5 percent rate. Risk drops as the fixed percentage decreases. In fact, the 5 percent rate shows the lowest risk of any stop. What that really means is that most of the other stop tests are probably equivalent to an 8 percent fixed percentage stop (based on the average loss).

Average True Range   The true range is the highest of:

* The current high price minus the low.
* The absolute value of the current high minus the previous close.
* The absolute value of the current low minus the previous close.

The average true range is just an average of the true range over time. The idea behind the three computations is to include any price gaps from day to day when computing the high-low trading range.

I used a 21-trading day (about one month) average and a two multiplier with the stop below the current low. Trail the stop upward. I chose these values so that they were the same as the volatility test (an apples to apples comparison). Here is the formula for the ATR stop:

* Stop price = Current low – (2 × ATR)

The stop cuts profits by 66 percent compared to the benchmark, but only slices risk by 13 percent. If those two numbers were reversed, then you would have something to brag about.

Volatility   A volatility stop is similar to the ATR stop except I use the high-low price range in place of the true range. Trail the stop upward.

* Stop price = Current low – (2 × (H – L))

The test results are similar to the ATR except that the average profit/ loss drops by $3 a trade (from $79 to $76), but risk drops a bit more.

In actual trading, I use a volatility stop based on 22 trading days instead of the 21 tested here. In a different test using my actual trades, I found that the volatility stop gave results superior to both the ATR stop and standard deviation stop (where standard deviation replaces the ATR).

Chandelier   The chandelier stop is an apt name for a stop that hangs below the highest high price. It has a formula similar to the ATR and volatility stops, namely,

* Stop price = Current high – (3 × ATR)

The average true range uses 21 trading days in the average and a three multiplier hangs from current high price. Trail the stop upward.

Despite being highly acclaimed by some, the stop performs worse than almost all of the other stops. Profits drop by 70 percent, but risk drops by only 14 percent when compared to buy and hold. Only the 5 percent fixed percentage stop makes fewer dollars per trade.

Top Stop Exit I learned about the top stop exit from an article cleverly titled "Top Stop Exit" (Knapp, 2008). He writes, "The Top Stop exit approach is a type of 'trailing' profit target. If the stock makes a new high in a long position, for example, the exit level will jump up. When the stock falls or enters a temporary consolidation, the profit target will drop."

Here are the five rules I used.

1. Enter a trade in the normal manner using the moving average crossover system, which is the same as for the other stop tests.
2. Exit the trade if price reaches 4.5 times the 14-day average true range plus the absolute value of today's closing price minus yesterday's close.
3. If today's close is the highest of the prior 20 trading days, then raise the target price by the difference between today's close and yesterday's close.
4. If today's close is *not* the highest of the prior 20 trading days, then lower the target price by the same amount (the difference between today's close and yesterday's close).
5. If this is *not* the *pure top stop exit* test, then sell the stock upon a moving average crossover as in other tests. If it *is* the pure top stop exit, then disable the moving average crossover sell mechanism.

The target price floats above the current price, depending on whether or not it is the highest closing price over the past month.

The *pure top stop exit*, where the moving average crossover exit is disabled, profits increase, but so does the average loss. Table 3.4 shows a higher profit per trade: $124, but the highest average loss ($689).

The top stop exit with MA combines two types of exits: top stop and moving average crossover. Profits drop 62 percent but risk only drops 4 percent. That would be wonderful if the numbers were reversed.

WHAT I USE

The type of stop I use varies depending on the trading or investing style. For buy-and-hold, I do not use a stop. Why? Because I want to hold the stock for years and not have to worry about a "flash crash" taking the stock down to a penny (which actually happened in 2010 in some stocks) and cashing me out along the way. I can tolerate price making large swings on a longer-term basis.

I use a mental stop when day trading. I do not have time to log the stop with my broker and continually check to see if it has been hit. On heavily traded stocks, I have had to wait for minutes just to confirm that my buy or sell order went through. I do not need another delay.

For position or swing trades, market conditions determine the type of stop used. Before I place a stop, I check how close I can place a stop without worrying about being stopped out on normal price action. That means I use a volatility stop and avoid placing the stop closer than what it says.

Sometimes (often for lower priced stocks) using a volatility stop would create a loss that is much too large. I switch to a minor low, but make sure the price I use is below what other traders aim for (so that if they push the stock down to take out the stops, mine will be a bit lower). Sometimes, they take me out of the game anyway. And I always avoid round numbers (those ending in zero).

If I am expecting a trend change, then I will park the stop a penny behind the prior day's low. In mid-2010 when I expected the market to slide from bull to bear, I started cashing out my strongest positions, trying to maximize gains. I used this technique and raised the stop each day until the stock took me out. Fortunately, I caught many straight-line runs and gave back little profit when the trend reversed. For unusually tall candles, I cut the high-low range in half and use that as the stop level (a penny or two below the midpoint).

Sometimes a chart pattern has a consolidation region where a stop is a good fit. Those regions are tight, sideways price movements where the stock shows lots of price overlap from day to day. Figure 3.1 in April, below the arc, shows a tight consolidation region. Point J in Figure 3.2 (circled) also shows what a tight consolidation region looks like.

A double bottom, for example, might show such a region in one of the bottoms. These shelves (as they are called), make wonderful entry points. Place a stop below the consolidation region and buy as price rises above the region. The consolidation region will tend to support price and you can ride the stock as it moves higher to confirm the double bottom pattern.

- Use a volatility stop to gauge how close a stop can be.
- Tuck stops below a minor low but far enough away that others will not shoot for it.
- Tight consolidation regions make for good stop locations.

CHAPTER CHECKLIST

The chapter title is, Do Stops Work? The answer is complicated. One fund manager said that if you wanted to be stopped out, then use a stop. The tests showed that being stopped out means profits get whacked in half and yet the risk of loss does not diminish much. In other words, traders have to be selective in how they use stops.

Here are some tips to consider when using stops.

☐ What size gain is required to overcome a given loss? See Table 3.1.

☐ Hold time loss is the largest potential loss during a trade. See What Is Hold Time Loss?

☐ A mental stop is one kept in your head and not placed with a broker. Only seasoned traders should use mental stops. See Mental Stop: For Professionals Only!

☐ Avoid placing stops where other traders place theirs. See Minor High or Low Stop: A Good Choice.

☐ Avoid placing stops at round numbers (those ending in zero). See Squaring Off Round Numbers.

☐ Chart patterns represent good stop locations because they often act as future support and resistance areas. See Chart Pattern Stop: Too Costly?

☐ Measure the distance from the stop to the buy price to make sure it is not too far away. See Chart Pattern Stop: Too Costly?

☐ When price rises to a new high, place a stop directly below the prior minor low and below the moving average at that minor low. See Stopped by a Moving Average.

☐ Draw up-sloping trendlines along valleys, down-sloping trendlines along peaks. See The Truth About Trendlines.

☐ For other tips about trendlines, see The Truth About Trendlines.

☐ Use a trendline for stop placement. Trail a stop upward as price rises, beneath a trendline at the prior minor low. Tighten the stop if price moves sideways, forming a congestion region. See Trendline Stop.

☐ A Fibonacci stop is useful for straight-line runs where the prior minor low might be too far away from the current price. Set a stop below the 62 percent (or 67 percent, see below) retrace value. See Fibonacci Retrace Stop: Deal or Dud?

☐ Place a stop a penny or two below the 67 percent (not 62 percent) retrace of the prior move up. See Fibonacci Tests Contradiction.

☐ Fibonacci retracements offer no advantage over any other number as a turning point. See Fibonacci Tests Contradiction.

☐ A fixed percentage trailing stop uses a constant percentage below the *high water mark* as a stop price. See Fixed Percentage Trailing Stop.

☐ Learn how to calculate a volatility stop. See Volatility Stop.

☐ A volatility stop helps prevent a position from being stopped out on normal price fluctuations. See Volatility Stop.

☐ A chandelier stop hangs off the high price. See Chandelier Stop Leaves You Hanging.

☐ Table 3.4 shows the performance of various stop types.

☐ Stops cut profit more than they limit risk. See Results Summary.

☐ See Average True Range for details on calculating the true range.

☐ See Top Stop Exit for details on a trailing profit target stop.

☐ Use a volatility stop to determine how close to place a stop, how to hide the stop below a minor low where others cannot find it, and how tight consolidation regions make for good stop locations. See What I Use.

CHAPTER 4

Support and Resistance

I f you can correctly determine how far price is going to move and act on it, the riches on Wall Street can be yours. Support and resistance can help with that. I consider them some of the most important trading tools.

When price drops, it finds underlying support. It is like watching water tumble over a multi-tiered fountain. Water pools at one level (finding support) then spills over the rim and cascades down to the next pool (finding support at a lower level) before filling that pool and tumbling again. If the falling water (price) finds support strong enough in the pool, then it splashes upward (price rises).

In a rising price trend, a stock bumps up against overhead resistance. That is similar to a helium-filled balloon released inside a hotel with balconies looking out over the atrium. The balloon rises and bumps up against the bottom of a balcony then it is blown outward and continues rising up to the next balcony. If overhead resistance is strong enough, the balloon pops and falls back down.

Price can plow through support or resistance without reversing, without stalling, or price can move sideways for days, weeks, or even months before surging forward again. Such inconsistencies are what make finding valid support and resistance areas so difficult. That is also why traders rely on probability and statistics so heavily. There are no sure things in trading.

TYPES OF SUPPORT AND RESISTANCE

Like ice cream, support and resistance (SAR) comes in many flavors, and **Figure 4.1** shows examples. On the top left , price bumps up against overhead resistance twice in January 2009 and once in June as shown by the horizontal line. This is an example of resistance at a minor high.

During January and February 2009, price finds support at about 52 (minor low support), but it does not last long. Price burns its way through and tumbles. Along the way down, price gaps lower. On the way back up, gap resistance repulses price in late March (F), forcing it lower, but only temporarily.

As price rises, it follows a trendline higher. The trendline acts as support. At 50 and 60, both round numbers, price finds support and resistance at those levels.

Notice that at point A price runs into underlying support and forms a minor low. At B, near the same price level, price hits a ceiling of overhead resistance. At C, that resistance is now support. Overhead resistance can become underlying support and vice versa.

* Resistance can become support that can become resistance.

FIGURE 4.1   Price shows various types of support and resistance.

MEASURED MOVE SUPPORT AND RESISTANCE

Before I discuss the various tests used to measure support and resistance, look at turns DAEF. Point D begins the move down from a small peak. It bottoms at A, bounces up to E before continuing lower to F. The DAEF move forms a measured move down chart pattern. The idea behind a measured move down is that the length of the first leg (DA) will approximate the length of the second leg (EF). The duration of the two legs is also similar (in theory).

* The first leg of a well-behaved measured move approximates the time and price move of the second leg.

There is also a measured move up chart pattern that applies to upward price trends. It has two rising legs with a small correction between the two legs. See my book, *Encyclopedia of Chart Patterns* (Wiley, 2005), for more information on these two patterns.

The reason I am discussing measured moves is because of what happens *after* the pattern ends. What does price do then? **Table 4.1** provides the answer. The term, *corrective phase*, is the retrace from A to E.

For example, in Figure 4.1 we see that point B peaks in the corrective phase AE before price turns lower. In the measured moves I looked at, this happened 35 percent of the time (price stops within the corrective phase).

The numbers in Table 4.1 are additive. For example, if you wanted to know how often price stops rising below the top of the measured move down (that is, below point D), the answer is 16 percent + 35 percent + 31 percent, or 82 percent of the time in a bull market.

TABLE 4.1 Percentage of Time Price Stops in a Measured Move

Measured Move Up	Bull Market	Bear Market
Price stops above the corrective phase	19%	24%
Price stops within the corrective phase	35%	40%
Price stops below the corrective phase but above the MMU low	31%	19%
Price stops below the MMU low	15%	16%
Measured Move Down (Below)		
Price stops below the corrective phase	16%	20%
Price stops within the corrective phase	35%	52%
Price stops above the corrective phase but below the MMD high	31%	20%
Price stops above the MMD high	18%	8%

The numbers apply only to the first attempt price makes to cross the pattern. For example, point B is the first attempt, but point C is not.

Since measured moves appear frequently, knowing the probabilities of where price is likely to turn is invaluable.

- Price stops within the corrective phase of a measured move chart pattern 35 percent of the time in a bull market.

What other areas show support or resistance, and can we prove it? The following tests help determine where price is going to reverse. In the tests, I used 571 stocks, but removed those priced below $5 a share and stopped logging them when they filled my spreadsheet (about 65,500 samples). The ending date on all tests was June 1, 2010, but they started at various times. I found all peaks or valleys that were within 35 cents of each other. The 35-cent window is the maximum difference in which two peaks look near one another, at least on my computer screen. It is an arbitrary value.

MINOR HIGH RESISTANCE

Minor highs and minor lows are known areas contributing to support and resistance. Let us start with minor highs. **Figure 4.2** shows the test configuration. This test answers the question, how often does a minor high (peak) show resistance to future price movement?

For each peak, I counted the number of times that price stopped near the same level, and quit counting when price climbed above the top of the window (the top of the window being 35 cents above the high price in the first peak). Then I moved on to the next peak. The test began with data starting in January 1, 2000, finding 65,535 samples.

I found that 34 percent of the peaks showed overhead resistance at least once before price pushed above the resistance layer. In other words, one of every three peaks will show future resistance before price moves higher.

- Overhead resistance occurs at peaks 34 percent of the time.

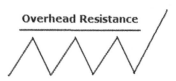

FIGURE 4.2   Test configuration: Overhead resistance at peaks.

VOLUME AT MINOR HIGH RESISTANCE

When I separated the results according to volume surrounding the first peak, I found no difference in future resistance. I computed the average volume two days before to two days after the peak and compared that to the prior month (21 trading days preceding 2 days before the peak so as not to overlap the periods). The ratio of the shorter average to the longer one determines whether the peak occurred on high or low volume.

Peaks that formed with above average volume had an average of 0.61 peaks that stopped near the same price (that is, they showed overhead resistance). Those peaks built on low volume showed an average of 0.60 peaks stopping near the same price in the future. In other words, a tie.

When I filtered the numbers, I found that peaks on very high volume (1.5 times the average) showed 0.63 peaks in the future compared to peaks on very low volume (0.5 times the average), which showed 0.69 peaks in the future.

In other words, peaks that have lower than average volume tend to exhibit more overhead resistance, but the differences are slight.

- Peaks with volume half the average tend to show more overhead resistance than those with 1.5 times the average volume.

MINOR LOW SUPPORT

Figure 4.3 shows the next test. I looked at valleys (minor lows) and counted the number of times price bottomed near the same price before digging through. I used data starting from January 2006 because I found so many samples that going back further was not necessary.

How often does a minor low support price? Answer: 33 percent of the time. In other words, one of every three valleys will show support at least once before price drops through.

- Valleys show support 33 percent of the time.

Underlying Support

FIGURE 4.3   Test configuration: Underlying support at valleys.

VOLUME AT MINOR LOW SUPPORT

In a manner the same as for peaks, I measured the volume surrounding valleys (two days before to two days after) and compared it to the average volume over the prior month. I found valleys that had low volume were more likely to show support than did valleys on high volume: 0.56 versus 0.52, respectively. Those numbers are the average valley counts.

If you look at very high or low volume, 1.5× to 0.5× of normal, the results widen. Those valleys on very low volume showed support 0.62 times on average compared to 0.52 for valleys on very high volume. A minor low forming on low volume is more likely to show support than those forming on high volume.

- Valleys with volume half the average tend to show more support than do those with volume 1.5 times the average.

MINOR HIGH SUPPORT

It may sound odd that peaks show support. When you think of a peak or minor high, the reason it is a peak is that price could not move higher because of overhead resistance. How then can a peak show support? **Figure 4.4** provides the answer. Price drops down from above (at B) and finds support at the price level of the first peak (A).

Peaks lending support is the scenario I tested next. For this test, I used data from stocks starting in June 1996 and ending in June 2010. The test excluded any stock below $5 and those without data extending back to mid-1996.

I found every peak in a seven-year window and followed each one for seven years, counting the number of times a valley stopped near the same peak compared to the number of times price punched through without showing support. **Table 4.2** shows the results.

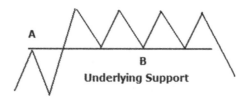

FIGURE 4.4   Test configuration: Peaks showing support.

TABLE 4.2 Percentage of Peaks Showing Support

Year 1	Year 2	Year 3	Year 4	Year 5	Year 6	Year 7
39%	45%	45%	46%	46%	42%	42%

For example, 39 percent of the time stocks showed support at the price of a peak sometime during a year after the peak formed. Support moved up to 45 and 46 percent in years 2 through 5 before easing back to 42 percent. This test shows that support does *not* diminish over time. Rather, it gets stronger (until after year 5, that is). This is the same result I found (using a different test) and discussed in my *Trading Classic Chart Patterns* book.

- Support gets stronger over time.

MINOR LOW RESISTANCE

Figure 4.5 shows the last test configuration using minor highs or lows. This test is as odd as the last one. I used the low price at a valley (A) to count how many peaks (B) stalled at that price. The test used the same 14-year window as in the prior test, and **Table 4.3** shows the results.

For example, 49 percent of the valleys set up resistance to upward price movement sometime in the following year. The table shows that resistance tends to remain potent throughout the seven-year cycle. More resistance comes in years 2 through 6 than in years 1 and 7. Overall, though, the trend is flat.

- The strength of overhead resistance tends to remain constant over time.

The following sections outline research discussed in my other books. Since this type of research is tedious, boring, and a huge pain to do, I just present the results instead of creating new ways to test for support and resistance.

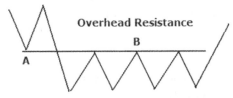

FIGURE 4.5 Test configuration: Overhead resistance from valleys.

TABLE 4.3 Percentage of Valleys Showing Resistance

Year 1	Year 2	Year 3	Year 4	Year 5	Year 6	Year 7
49%	52%	51%	50%	52%	51%	48%

GAPS SHOWING SUPPORT AND RESISTANCE

In my book, *Encyclopedia of Candlestick Charts* (Wiley, 2008), I explored rising and falling windows as they pertain to support and resistance. A rising window is a fancy way of saying gap in an upward price trend. A falling window is a gap in a declining price trend. Refer to that book for a discussion of the methods used to test for support and resistance in gaps.

My research found that gaps support price 20 percent of the time. That means price gaps up, and then returns to the gap and stops there one in five times. A gap also shows overhead resistance 25 percent of the time. Price gaps lower then tries to move higher, but halts somewhere within the gap once every four times.

- Gaps show support 20 percent of the time and resistance 25 percent of the time in a bull market.

MYTH: TALL CANDLE SUPPORT AND RESISTANCE

Do tall candles (tall bodies) show support or resistance halfway up the candle as some claim? No, based on research I conducted and discuss in my *Encyclopedia of Candlestick Charts* book. I found 41,301 tall-bodied candles that were twice the average height of the prior month, and measured how often a minor high or minor low stopped within the candle's body. A frequency distribution of the results, broken down into 10 percent increments of the candle's height, showed that "the middle of a tall candle showed no greater likelihood of exhibiting support or resistance than anywhere else in a tall candle." Another test using 15 years of data on candles four times the average height came to the same conclusion.

- The middle of a tall candle is no more likely to show support or resistance than any other part.

HORIZONTAL CONSOLIDATION REGIONS

I tore apart horizontal consolidation regions (HCRs) in *Trading Classic Chart Patterns*, so you can reference that book for the details. A HCR is just as it sounds, an area or zone of flat price movement. To qualify, the region must have at least three peaks or three valleys sharing the same price, and they should *not* be spread across the known galaxy.

I measured the effectiveness of HCRs by finding them from the trend start to the start of a chart pattern (on a time basis, and from the trend start to the top or bottom of a chart pattern on a price basis), when the breakout placed price in the path of the HCR.

For example, price started trending lower, formed a horizontal consolidation region, and then continued to a double bottom. When the chart pattern broke out upward, price climbed and reached the level of the HCR. I measured how often that type of behavior occurred and found the following.

- Support or resistance does not grow weaker over time. If the HCR was near the chart pattern breakout, price often pushed though nearby resistance or support. HCRs' ability to stop price movement increased for about a month and then oscillated up and down thereafter (for up to 530 days, with no real change).
- HCRs below a chart pattern were slightly better at stopping a decline than were HCRs above the chart pattern at stopping rises. With HCRs 70 days from the start of the chart pattern, they stopped price 47 percent (upward breakouts from the chart pattern) to 60 percent (downward breakouts) of the time.

  The strongest HCRs for downward breakouts were about a month away (67 percent stopped within the HCR) and for upward breakouts, 49 days showed the highest stopping power (50 percent stopped within the HCR).
- On a price basis, the further away the HCR is from a chart pattern, the weaker it is. For upward breakouts, the HCR stops price 48 percent of the time if the HCR is just 5 percent away, and this dwindles to 15 percent for HCRs 40 percent away.
- As a general guideline, an HCR with a 5 percent buffer surrounding it stops upward breakouts 41 percent of the time and downward breakouts 55 percent of the time.
- Long HCRs stop price better than do short ones. For upward breakouts, HCRs 7 days wide stop price 40 percent of the time, but those 70 days wide stop 58 percent of price movement.
- HCRs with average volume showed the best stopping power, not low or high volume HCRs.

ANOTHER LOOK AT ROUND NUMBERS

I remember trying to justify price stopping at round numbers and people jumped up and down on me, mathematically proving that numbers ending in zero were no more likely to show support or resistance than any other number. It may sound like bumblebees not being able to fly, theoretically, and yet we all know that they do. The *Trading Classic Chart Patterns* book examined round number SAR.

I found horizontal consolidation regions, and then computed how often those HCRs included a round number. Answer: 22 percent of the time.

• Price trends horizontally near a round number 22 percent of the time.

SUPPORT IN STRAIGHT-LINE RUNS

An article I read gave me an idea about searching for support and resistance in straight-line price runs. Testing the idea is one of the more boring aspects of writing this book, but I try to prove what I write. That is what makes my books different from others. I present new research or discuss existing techniques and prove their effectiveness. This section is part one of a two-part discussion of price behavior in straight-line runs.

I wanted to know how often a consolidation region in a straight-line run acts as support to price in the future. To simplify things, I am only interested in counting the first time price passes into a consolidation area and finds support.

Figure 4.6 shows an example of a straight-line run that starts at L (February) and leads to consolidation region A (circled). To the right of that area, which I show as the region between the two horizontal lines, is a spike at B that finds support (meaning it stops between the two lines). Point B is the first time that price drops to A. Region A marks a valid support area.

Price moves up to consolidation region C. Notice that price drops right through region C at D. However, circle E sits on top of C and pokes through the top of the region at J. Thus, circle C is also a valid support area because of the downward price spikes that stop at J.

Look at circle E. I include the F spikes since I consider it as one long consolidation area. Price at G does not find support between the two horizontal lines because it keeps dropping until reaching area A. The EF area does not support price.

Notice that price at area K *does* find support at EF, but, since it is not the first time that price drops into or through area EF, I ignore it. I am only

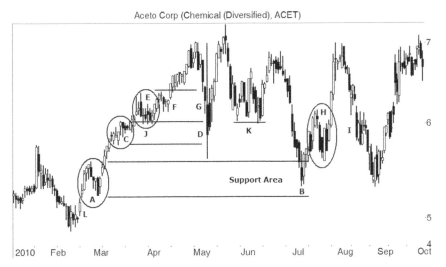

Aceto Corp (Chemical (Diversified), ACET)

FIGURE 4.6   Support appears in a straight-line run.

interested in finding the *first* example of a congestion region acting as support in a straight-line run.

Area H is another congestion region in a straight-line run that begins at B. Notice how price pauses at I. Thus, area H shows support when price drops into the area at I. The support is not strong since price only hesitates for a week before continuing lower, but area H is still a support zone.

How often do areas like A, C, and EF support price? To answer that, I looked at 231 stocks on the daily scale using data from January 2009 to February 16, 2011. That is just over 450 years of daily price data.

I found that the first and lowest consolidation area acted as support 183 out of 215 times, or 85 percent. In Figure 4.6, the area I am referring to is A because it is the first and lowest consolidation area.

The next lowest area is C and price finds support 128 times in 174 tries, or 74 percent of the time. The third and last congestion area finds support 56 out of 81 tries, or 69 percent of the time.

The numbers suggest that the lower price drops, the higher the chance that it will find support in a straight-line run.

- Price finds support in a straight-line run between 69 percent (third lowest support area) and 85 percent (first lowest support area) of the time.

RESISTANCE IN STRAIGHT-LINE RUNS

I cataloged resistance in straight-line runs just as I did with support. Only this time I used 300 stocks to find enough samples over the same two-year duration. **Figure 4.7** shows an example.

Price forms a small resistance zone at A, reaches it at B, and stalls. At C, a larger resistance area forms, but this is a loose looking one. At D, price just breezes past C as if the resistance area were not there. At E, another resistance area lasts just a few days and yet it was powerful enough to repel prices at F.

Testing for resistance in a downward straight-line run finds that the first area (A), shows overhead resistance 177 out of 258 times, or 69 percent. Area C shows future resistance 66 out of 90 times or 74 percent. Zone E is rare in a bull market. I only found 19 samples out of 25 tries, or 76 percent, where the area acted as resistance.

- In a straight-line run downward, price sets up future resistance between 69 percent (first highest resistance area) and 76 percent (third highest resistance area) of the time.

FIGURE 4.7   A straight-line run down forms resistance to an upward price trend.

Let me emphasize that just because a congestion area appears in a straight-line run is no reason to believe that price will reverse there. I did not check for a *lasting* reversal, only that price paused there, finding either support or resistance in the consolidation area.

SAR SUMMARY

Table 4.4 is perhaps the most important one in this book. It details how often price patterns show support and resistance, sorted by the percentage. The numbers are for bull markets only.

TABLE 4.4 Support and Resistance Summary

Description	Effectiveness	Reference
Consolidation areas showing support in straight-line runs.	69% to 85%	Support in Straight-Line Runs
Consolidation areas showing resistance in straight-line runs.	69% to 76%	Resistance in Straight-Line Runs
Horizontal consolidation regions showing support	55%	Horizontal Consolidation Regions
Valleys showing resistance	48% to 52%	Table 4.3
Horizontal consolidation regions showing resistance	41%	Horizontal Consolidation Regions
Peaks showing support	39% to 46%	Table 4.2
Corrective phase of a measured move up or down stopping power	35%	Table 4.1
Peaks showing resistance	34%	Minor High Resistance
Valleys showing support	33%	Minor Low Support
Gaps showing resistance	25%	Gaps Showing Support and Resistance
Round number support and resistance	22%	Another Look at Round Numbers
Gaps showing support	20%	Gaps Showing Support and Resistance
Tall candles do not show unusual support or resistance	True	Myth: Tall Candle Support and Resistance
Peaks with below average volume show more resistance	True	Volume at Minor High Resistance
Valleys with below average volume show more support	True	Volume at Minor Low Support
Support gets stronger over time	True	Table 4.2
Strength of overhead resistance remains constant over time	True	Table 4.3

CHAPTER CHECKLIST

At the opening of this chapter, I wrote, "If you can correctly determine how far price is going to move and act on it, the riches on Wall Street can be yours."

One way to find the limits of moves is to use support and resistance. However, Table 4.4 shows that support and resistance only works a fraction of the time. That is a problem when depending on a minor high to set up overhead resistance because it happens only once every three trades. How then are we to make money in stocks?

The next chapter tries to answer that question by offering experience in the form of dozens of tips. Hopefully, those tips can begin to close the gap between losses and profits.

Before we get there, though, here is a checklist of the important findings from this chapter.

☐ Resistance can become support that can become resistance. See Types of Support and Resistance.

☐ The first leg of a well-behaved measured move approximates the time and price move of the second leg. See Measured Move Support and Resistance.

☐ Price stops within the corrective phase of a measured move chart pattern 35 percent of the time in a bull market. See Table 4.1.

☐ Overhead resistance occurs at peaks 34 percent of the time. See Minor High Resistance.

☐ Peaks with volume half the average tend to show more overhead resistance than those with 1.5 times the average volume. See Volume at Minor High Resistance.

☐ Valleys show support 33 percent of the time. See Minor Low Support.

☐ Valleys with volume half the average tend to show more support than do those with volume 1.5 times the average. See Volume at Minor Low Support.

☐ Table 4.2 shows that support gets stronger over time.

☐ Table 4.3 shows that the strength of overhead resistance tends to remain constant over time.

☐ Gaps show support 20 percent of the time and resistance 25 percent of the time in a bull market. See Gaps Showing Support and Resistance.

☐ The middle of a tall candle is no more likely to show support or resistance than any other part. See Myth: Tall Candle Support and Resistance.

☐ See Horizontal Consolidation Regions for details about the stopping power of those regions.

☐ Price trends horizontally near a round number 22 percent of the time. See Another Look at Round Numbers.

☐ Price finds support in a straight-line run between 69 and 85 percent of the time. See Support in Straight-Line Runs.

☐ In a straight-line run downward, price sets up future resistance between 69 and 76 percent of the time. See Resistance in Straight-Line Runs.

☐ Table 4.4 shows a summary of support and resistance at technical features.

CHAPTER 5

45 Tips Every Trader Should Know

After 30 years of taking money out of the hands of professionals on Wall Street and newbies on Main Street, I have learned tips that every trader and investor should know. These I describe below. I refer to them in other chapters, so here is a brief tutorial.

1. Timing the Exit: The 2B Rule

In Victor Sperandeo's book, *Trader Vic—Methods of a Wall Street Master* (Wiley, 1991), he discusses three principles to determine when the primary trend changes. On principle two, he introduces a rule that has come to be known as 2B.

In the 2B pattern, when price tests (rises near to) a prior minor high and fails to continue rising, look for price to drop. That may sound as if I am saying, if price does not rise, it drops, but this is valuable information. I will discuss an example in a moment.

The same applies to valleys. If price drops to a minor low and fails to continue moving lower and then rises above the prior low, there is a decent chance of a trend change.

Figure 5.1 shows an example in Boeing on the daily scale. Price peaks at A, in June 2009. When price attempts to push above this peak three months later at B, it fails in a 2B pattern. Price tumbles to D and then recovers to C where it stalls again—another 2B—but this time forms a peak that looks laced with indecision about moving higher. Price tanks for three days to E before the uptrend resumes.

FIGURE 5.1 Examples of the 2B rule where price reverses on the test of a prior high and low.

Point I is another 2B test of A, but this time price moves above peak A. That is fine. Price on the test can fall a bit short, rise a bit above, or hit the price of the prior peak exactly. What is important is that price attempts to post higher highs, but fails.

Peaks CIH mark the boundaries of a head-and-shoulders top chart pattern. In fact, many chart patterns depend on the 2B rule. Double tops and bottoms, triple tops and bottoms, even head-and-shoulders follow the 2B rule, at least to some degree.

Look at valley F on the lower left of the chart. Price attempts to make a lower valley at G but fails. This is the 2B rule as it applies to bottoms. You may find the bottom 2B useful for swing and day trading.

Sperandeo gives these specifications for 2Bs at peaks, but the same applies to valleys.

- On short-term highs, look for a reversal in a day or two. Points B, H, and I are examples.
- For intermediate-term highs, the 2B should reverse in three to five days.
- Long-term trends (major turning points) take longer, 7 to 10 days for price to weaken.

- Look for low to average volume on the attempt at a new high, but high volume when price begins heading lower.
- If price rises above a 2B, then cover a short position.

My use of the 2B is unusual because it depends on intuition and experience. Often my inner voice speaks up and says, "Price is going to reverse." If I act on that notion, I can exit near the peak. Price may not drop far before moving to a new high, but many times, I have had the trend change and watched a major move down unfold. I felt fortunate to exit when I did.

The 2B pattern is most useful for swing trades where you are playing the intermediate-term trend. Sperandeo says that it works about half the time for day trades, but better than that for intermediate-term trades. My feeling is it depends on the type of market.

If you are in a raging bull market, then the 2B rule will lead to diminished gains (when you cash out prematurely). If the market is weak or if it is in a trading range, then the 2B rule can work miracles as well as your favorite religious icon.

- If price stalls near an old high or low, it could reverse.

2. Busted Patterns for Profit

My books, *Getting Started in Chart Patterns* and *Visual Guide to Chart Patterns,* discuss busted patterns and provide a limited set of performance statistics, so I will not test them here nor give a complete discussion of them. However, a brief review will help those not familiar with busted patterns.

I coined the term *busted pattern* to define when price stages a breakout in one direction and then flips around to breakout in a new direction. You see this type of behavior in many patterns, especially those that tend to narrow over time (ascending, descending, and symmetrical triangles), but it also happens in double bottoms, tops, and other patterns, as well.

Look at inset E of **Figure 5.2**. The box represents any chart pattern. This one has an upward breakout, but price does not rise far before reversing. When price *closes* below the *bottom* of the chart pattern, it busts the upward breakout, sending traders holding the stock to the vault for another pound of fifties to cover their losses. The drop after an upward bust tends to be a powerful one, but each situation is different.

Inset F shows a similar situation as it applies to downward breakouts. Price closes below the chart pattern, staging a breakout, and dropping less than 10 percent (10 percent is an arbitrary number applied to either breakout direction, but one I have used in testing and found it works well). Price reverses course and heads back into the pattern as if executing a pullback, but then price zips out the top of the chart pattern, staging another

AC Moore Arts and Crafts (Retail (Special Lines), ACMR)

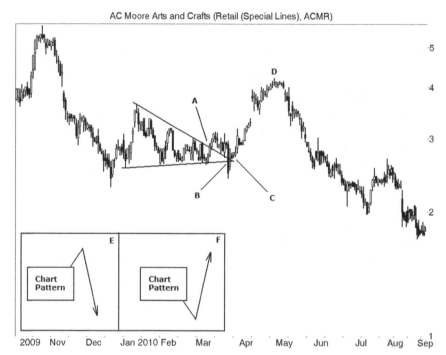

FIGURE 5.2 A symmetrical triangle double busts.

breakout. When price *closes* above the *top* of the chart pattern, it busts the pattern. The upward breakout will tend to be a powerful one.

The figure also shows an example of a double-busted symmetrical triangle. The breakout is upward (A) when price closes above the top trendline. Price returns to the upper trendline boundary just over a week later.

Then something unusual happens. Price closes below the bottom of the chart pattern at B. This busts the upward breakout for the first time and creates a new breakout direction—downward. But the downward direction also reverses and breaks out upward at C. Price rises far enough to close above the top of the triangle, busting it for the second time before topping out at D.

I have found that double busting is rare in chart patterns (only 7 percent for symmetrical triangles, which bust 42 percent of the time), but it does occur. When they do bust (single, double, and more than double busts, combined), they tend to slightly underperform their non-busted counterparts, but that depends on how it is measured. Patterns that only bust once, for example, significantly outperform their non-busted counterparts.

Busted chart patterns are rare, and not on the radar screens of the usual pattern traders. Once a regular pattern fails, people look elsewhere for another trade, leaving the stock free to move in a new direction.

It is possible that the smart money (hedge funds, institutional traders, and so on that have a large stake in a stock) lets a breakout in one direction occur then jumps in and pushes price in the new direction, forcing a bust. When that happens, others join the busted trend and away price moves.

Look for busted chart patterns as a way to make easy money. Well, maybe not that easy. They may take the shape of a confirmed double top that drops less than 10 percent before turning into a firework and rocketing above the top of the chart pattern (which is an example of a busted double top).

It may help if the busted direction aligns with the general market trend. For example, if a double bottom breaks out *upward* in a *bear* market, that is a countertrend move. If price then throws back to the breakout and continues lower, below the bottom of the chart pattern, the new direction aligns with the bearish market trend.

When the stock, industry, and market all align, you will tend to have more successful trades than if any one or more of those directions do not align. In short, trade with the trend.

- Busted patterns are those that breakout, but do not move far before reversing and breaking out in a new direction.
- Busted patterns slightly underperform regular chart patterns.
- Stock performance improves if the busted direction aligns with the price trend shown by the industry and general market.

3. What I Use: Fibonacci Retracements

When discussing stops in Chapter 3, I dug into Fibonacci retraces, tested it, and found a contradiction. One test said it saw turns at 61 percent (close to 62 percent) and 50 percent (but not 38 percent), and the other test found no significance to those three turning points.

I use Fibonacci retracements as I terrorize the markets because I believe it adds value. I have traded a Fibonacci retrace several times and made a lot of money on each trade.

When trying to predict how far price is going to drop, I will chart three retracement levels: 38, 50, and 62 percent.

Figure 5.3 shows an example. This daily chart uses the linear scale instead of the logarithmic one that I use most often. On the linear scale, the horizontal lines should be the same distance apart.

Charting programs often include a Fibonacci tool that will calculate and show retracements and extensions. I wrote such a tool for my homebrew program. Begin by selecting two major turning points. In this example, that is A and B. A is the launch point for the move up to peak B.

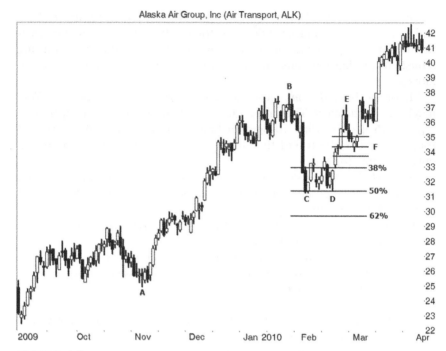

FIGURE 5.3   Three retracement levels appear on the daily chart, linear scale.

I want to know how far price is likely to drop, so I calculate 38, 50, and 62 percent of the prior up move and draw three horizontal lines at those levels. That is what I show on the chart.

In this example, price at C retraces to the 50 percent level before rebounding. If your software does not have a tool to draw those lines for you, here is the math for the 50 percent line. Price at A bottoms at 24.91, and at B it peaks at 37.95. Half of that distance is (37.95 – 24.91) ÷ 2 or 6.52, and when added to the low at A, the retrace is 31.43.

At F, I show another example of price retracing 38, 50, and 62 percent of the move from D to E. This time the stock bottoms midway between 50 and 62 percent.

4. Myth: Fibonacci Extensions Work!

Fibonacci extensions go the other way. They help predict the extent of the move above or below a turning point. Using Figure 5.3 as an example, take the height of swing AB and multiply it by 38 percent then add it to the high price to get the 38 percent extension. That turns out to be 42.91, near the high on the chart.

You can also subtract 38 percent of the height from the low price to get the downward projection: 19.95. I read of one user who preferred a 27 percent extension and another who uses 62 percent instead of 38 percent. My guidance is to use the one that works best for your markets.

The inset in **Figure 5.4** shows how they are supposed to work. Price turns at E and moves higher to F. If you measure the EF move and project it upward from F using what is called a Fibonacci extension, you should get point G. Point G is where the move ends.

The extension can be 38, 50, 62 percent, and so on. Software programs often show the EF move as 100 percent and point G might be 162 percent (or 62 percent longer than the EF move).

I programmed my computer to find the four turns (EFHG) shown in the figure and compared the EF move to FG. The test used 926 stocks and found 31,919 samples from March 2000 to April 2011. That period included two bear markets and two bull ones.

Figure 5.4 shows a frequency distribution of the extension (the FG move) as a percentage of the EF move for both bull and bear markets.

In a bull market, for example, 8 percent of the samples showed an FG move of between 0 and 10 percent. In another example, 7 percent of the samples reached the 15 percent target. That means the FG move was just 15 percent of the EF move.

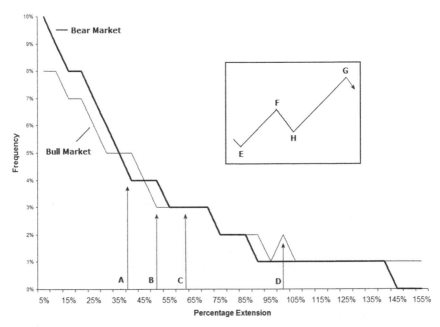

FIGURE 5.4   The chart shows no spikes at common Fibonacci extension numbers.

The longer the extension, the fewer the number of stocks showed price reaching that far.

If Fibonacci extensions worked, then I would expect to see a cluster of samples at the more popular numbers, such as 38 percent (point A), 50 percent (B), and 62 percent (C). The chart does not show any spikes at those levels.

However, at 100 percent, point D, we see a slight increase in the number of samples. In other words, 2 percent of the samples had the FG move matching the EF move compared to 1 percent of samples on either side of 100 percent. It is as if traders decided to cash in their profits once they doubled their money. Even so, the increase is slight. Due to round off, the actual change for 95, 100, and 105 percent bins are a frequency of 1.5, 1.6, and 1.3 percent, respectively. That is hardly a rousing endorsement.

For the data I used and results found, it appears that Fibonacci extensions are no more accurate than randomly choosing any price as a possible turning point.

- Fibonacci extensions are no more accurate than any other tool for determining where price might reverse.

5. Is Indicator Divergence a Dud?

Divergence is a complicated sounding name for a technique that is not complex, but you have to be careful using it. I show an example in **Figure 5.5**, which is a daily chart of Anadarko Petroleum on the top half of the panel. On the bottom half, I show a 16-period look back on the relative strength index (RSI).

At B, price forms two peaks at the same level, but the indicator at A shows a second peak below the first. The indicator points the way lower, suggesting a coming price drop.

At C, a similar situation develops, only this time it is bullish. Price flatlines but the indicator (D) forms a higher valley, pointing the way upward. Price moves higher during the next month.

Using the RSI, I have found that peaks or valleys about a month apart provide the most reliable results. If price is trending upward, then look for divergence along the peaks in both charts. If price trends down, then look for divergence along the valleys. That is the only tricky thing about divergence. Do not compare the peaks on one chart with valleys on the other, and do not look at the valleys in an upward trend or peaks in a downward trend.

- Divergence hints of a coming price turn. Look for divergence along the peaks in a rising price trend and along the valleys in a falling trend.

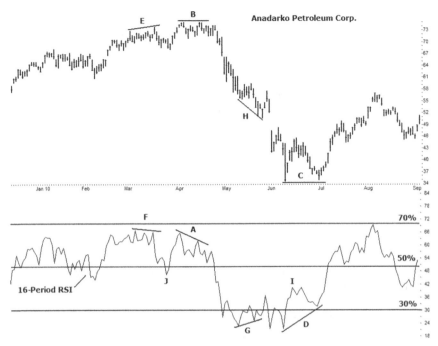

FIGURE 5.5 Bullish and bearish divergence appears when the indicator points one way and the stock another.

I read somewhere that you should ignore RSI divergence unless it is at the extremes, such as above 70 or below 30. Figure 5.5 shows that it works regardless in this example, but the caution makes sense. The overbought (above 70) or oversold (below 30) regions on the RSI are telling that the stock is trading at unusual levels and apt to reverse. Divergence highlights when conditions are favorable for a reversal, but it does not say when it will occur.

If divergence happens mid range (between 30 and 70), then it is more likely to be false. Price will just continue moving up or down. Thus, it is best if divergence occurs at or near the overbought and oversold regions.

- On the RSI indicator, look for divergence when it signals an overbought or oversold condition (locations where a price reversal is more likely) with two turning points about a month to six weeks apart.

Just because the two charts diverge is no reason to believe that price will make a large move. Consider points E and F in Figure 5.5. Price forms a higher peak, but the RSI shows a slightly lower peak. Price drops, but not very far.

Point G is another example. The indicator says price should move higher while at H, price is making a lower valley. Then price bounces but not far before resuming the downward price trend. Even though the indicator said the stock was oversold, that did not prevent price from continuing to drop. Indicators are like everything else in technical analysis. Sometimes they work and sometimes they do not.

Testing Divergence To test divergence, I programmed my computer to find it in the relative strength index (RSI). I used 994 stocks from January 1995 to September 2010 and found 19,294 examples of divergence. I filtered those by excluding divergence that did not begin from the oversold or overbought regions and separated the results into bull and bear markets. The bear markets were from March 24, 2000, to October 10, 2002, and October 12, 2007, to March 6, 2009, and the bull markets were everything outside of those ranges.

In each stock, I found all peaks or valleys that were the highest high or lowest low from 8 days before to 8 days after the peak or valley (17 days total). I assumed a person would buy the stock at the opening price on day 9, the nearest open after the search for the peak or valley ended. I excluded all peaks or valleys that were not between three weeks and 2.5 months apart. Experience has shown that those peaks or valleys between a month and two months apart give the best divergence. That may or may not be true. I did not test different periods.

When price formed two tops or bottoms, I looked at the RSI values for those two dates. Often they corresponded to (or were close to) peaks or valleys in the RSI as well. I only concerned myself with the values of the RSI on those dates, not whether they showed turning points in the indicator. This could be a criticism of the study since most people look for defined peaks and valleys in the RSI as well as price. A check of various stocks with the RSI plotted did not show this to be a problem. When price bottomed, so did the RSI; when price peaked, so did the RSI.

Table 5.1 shows the results as average gains over time. For example, three weeks after price formed the second bottom in a bull market and after the RSI showed bullish divergence, the stocks had gains averaging 7.0 percent. That compares to an average gain of 0.5 percent for the S&P 500 index over the same periods. In all cases, stocks showing bullish divergence outperformed the S&P. That is as good as it gets.

Look at the next set of rows down. If bullish divergence worked, stocks would show larger gains or smaller losses than the S&P 500 index in a bear market. Instead, stocks after three weeks showed losses averaging 1.2 percent compared to losses of 0.2 percent for the index. After a month, the losses were 2.2 percent for stocks versus 0.9 percent for the

TABLE 5.1 Results of Divergence Tests

Security	Divergence	Market	3 Weeks	1 Month	2 Months	3 Months
Stocks	Bullish	Bull	7.0%	8.0%	9.7%	11.6%
S&P 500			0.5%	1.2%	3.0%	5.3%
Stocks	Bullish	Bear	−1.2%	−2.2%	−3.2%	−4.9%
S&P 500			−0.2%	-0.9%	−3.3%	−5.9%
Stocks	Bearish	Bull	4.1%	4.3%	5.3%	6.6%
S&P 500			0.3%	0.6%	1.7%	2.7%
Stocks	Bearish	Bear	0.3%	−0.3%	−2.9%	−5.5%
S&P 500			−0.9%	−1.8%	−3.9%	−6.4%

index. After two months, the numbers are essentially a tie. Only after three months do stocks showing bullish divergence outperform the index.

If bearish divergence worked, stocks would perform *worse* than the index. That is not what the table shows. In all cases, regardless of the bull or bear market, the stocks outperformed the index.

- Only bullish divergence works and only in a bull market.

The performance numbers in Table 5.1 are *averages*. Large numbers can skew the average upward. Since we know that bullish divergence only works in a bull market, how often does each stock showing bullish divergence beat the performance of the S&P 500 index? Answer: between 45 percent (for the three-week test) and 48 percent (after two months).

- Bullish divergence fails to beat the market more often than it works.

6. Shallow Divergence and the RSI

Do shallow divergence swings lead to more powerful moves? I show an example of that in Figure 5.5 at point I. Bullish divergence is at C and D. When point I, which is the highest peak between the start and end of the divergence remains below 50 percent, it is supposed to signal a more powerful move. That is for bullish divergence. For *bearish* divergence, a swing above 50 percent (a shallow dip) means a more powerful move.

Use your imagination here, and pretend that the combination of F and A (assuming it peaked over 70) shows bearish divergence between E and B. The drop to J, which bottoms below 50 percent, suggests a weak move down. That is the theory, but does it work? Yes, but only sometimes. **Table 5.2** shows the numbers.

TABLE 5.2 Results of Shallow Divergence Percentage Totals**

Divergence	Market	Less Than 50	More Than 50	Result
Bullish	Bull	36.1%*	36.5%	Hurts
Bullish	Bear	−3.8%*	−17.5%	Helps
Bearish	Bull	18.5%	22.2%*	Hurts
Bearish	Bear	−7.6%	−9.4%*	Helps

* Less than 50 (bullish divergence) or more than 50 (bearish divergence) are best for this type of divergence.

** The percentages are the sum of the gains after 3 weeks, and months 1, 2, and 3.

Instead of showing a large table of percentages over time, I summed the percentages for each period (3 weeks + 1 + 2 + 3 months) and those are the percentages that appear in the table. This makes it easier to see if shallow indicator swings work best.

For example, the percentage change over the four sampling periods in a bull market for stocks showing bullish divergence is 36.1 percent when the indicator remained below 50. This compares to a total of 36.5 percent for those cases in which the indicator climbed above 50. In other words, the technique did not work in this scenario, since we expected to see a larger percentage gain if the indicator remained below 50. The next row down, bullish divergence/bear market, shows better performance by losing substantially less in a bear market.

Look at the last row. During bearish divergence in a bear market, performance should show a larger loss if the indicator remains above 50 (a shallow dip). Indeed, it does when stocks show losses of 9.4 percent (indicator over 50) compared to losses of just 7.6 percent (indicator below 50).

- If the RSI indicator remains shallow during divergence, performance improves, but only in a bear market.

7. Good Eggs: Indicator Failure Swings

The poor performance of divergence calls into question how failure swings perform. Failure swings are small versions of bullish or bearish divergence, seen on the RSI and other indicator charts.

Figure 5.6 shows an example using the RSI chart on Mueller. Failure swings look like small M or W shaped turns, like that circled at A. Other bullish and bearish failure swings appear in the inset, taken from the same chart, but over different months than that shown. Their appearance varies, but you will know a failure swing when you see it.

I drew two vertical lines on the chart to show how the failure swing at A lines up with price. In this example, you would not have much time to find the failure swing before price zipped up, but the longer term move

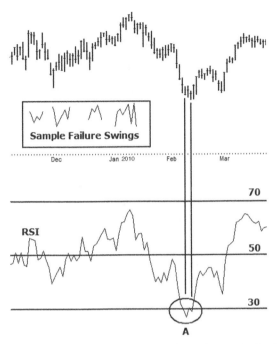

FIGURE 5.6   Failure swings are small M or W shaped turns in the indicator.

suggested the turn in February was a lasting one (since price moved higher well into March).

I did not test failure swings, so I do not know how well they perform. However, I have used them with success in my trading, so I consider them valuable.

The theory behind failure swings is that they should appear when the indicator is in the overbought or oversold regions. Again, you are looking for price that is ready to reverse. Another tip is to find patterns where the right bottom is above the left one, as is the case at A. That is supposed to show a more bullish move. For tops, look for a lower right peak. Neither of the M failure swings in the inset look compelling, but you can find them on your charts for the indicator of your choice and see how price behaves.

- Look for small M or W shaped turns beginning from the overbought or oversold regions. It is best if the right peak is below—or the right valley is above—the left one.

8. Flat Base Entry Pattern

The flat base pattern is like a rash that will not go away: I will mention it again in this trilogy. The pattern is an easy way for finding stocks that climb not just by 20 percent, but double and triple in price. That will not happen every time, of course, and it can take an extended holding period to reach those goals.

Figure 5.7 shows JetBlue Airways on the weekly chart using the linear price scale. That means the vertical distance from 2 to 3 is the same as that shown between 15 and 16. On a logarithmic scale, the distances are different.

Price moved horizontally after crashing on the runway in the summer of 2008. From mid-2009 onward, price has stayed between 5 and 7 as if waiting for clearance to begin the takeoff roll. The figure is an example of a flat base pattern, where price moves sideways for an extended period.

The ideal flat base pattern has a flat top and a flat bottom with narrow up and down price fluctuations. The stock moves sideways for months or even years until the breakout comes. That is when price closes above the top of the pattern. Even then, price may not fly up to where the air is too thin to breathe without bottled oxygen. Rather, the flight will take the

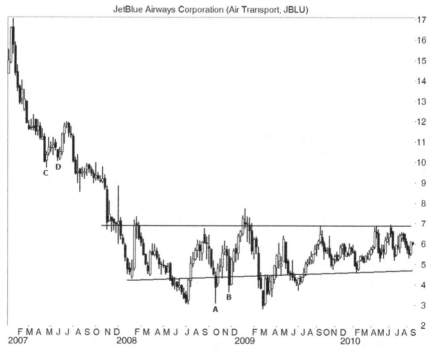

FIGURE 5.7   A flat base appears in JetBlue.

shape of most climbs, moving higher and then retracing before soaring to the next higher level.

Spotting a flat base can take some imagination. As Figure 5.7 shows, neither the top nor the bottom is perfectly flat. If you were walking on this in bare feet, you might suffer puncture wounds (I had one person e-mail me a picture of him walking (running) on red-hot charcoal. I think he is wearing prosthetics now).

Redrawing the chart without the large decline from 17 makes the chart look like a moonscape: a jagged landscape infested with sharp peaks and valleys and difficult to recognize as a flat base.

For pattern recognition, using the weekly or monthly chart and linear scale helps compress the vertical price movement when the stock makes a large swing.

- Use the linear scale to look for flat bases.
- Switch to the weekly or monthly charts.
- Price will be irregularly shaped, but moving horizontally for months or years, often bounded on the bottom and top by an invisible floor and ceiling.

Once price pierces the top of the trading range, then that could be the buy signal. Research the company to understand the growth prospects and why price is moving up. Take a position if you like what you discover. If the stock is going to double or triple, you will have plenty of time to make a purchase. Often, price will return to the top of the range, so that will provide another entry point.

You might want to marry entry with a close above the 30-week simple moving average. That will not guarantee success, but it may help you select stocks that are ready to move up instead of beginning to trade horizontally at a slightly higher range.

9. Identifying and Trading Gaps

I wrote an article on gaps for a magazine and soon, someone posted an illegal copy of it on the Internet. On one website alone, the article had over 1,200 downloads. That suggests traders love gaps. I prefer women.

The last chapter mentioned that gaps work as support or resistance areas about 20 to 25 percent of the time. That is weak performance. However, the *type* of gap provides a clue to future price behavior.

Area Gaps   On the daily chart, various types of gaps appear regularly. I show an ideal situation in **Figure 5.8**. Price churns sideways in a loose-looking consolidation region where an area gap forms. Area gaps occur

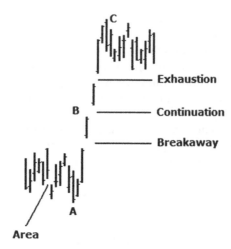

FIGURE 5.8   The various gap types appear as a stock moves higher.

frequently in congestion regions, but they *close* quickly. *Closing* means price retraces enough to cover the area exposed by the gap. In this example, price closes the gap the next day. The average time to close an area gap is three days based on a sample of 484 area gaps in 97 stocks from 1991 to 2004.

Volume tends to be high on the day price gaps higher, but drops back to normal in a day or two in an area gap. Price forms a curl as it fills the gap, and that means no new highs or lows appear after this gap. In other words, price continues moving sideways.

- Area gaps appear in congestion regions on high volume, but price fills the gap quickly and continues consolidating.

Breakaway Gaps   Breakaway gaps occur as price leaves a congestion area, starting a new price trend. Volume tends to be high and remains above average for several days. Price continues to make new highs, and it takes an average of 136 days in a bull market to close an upward breakout gap, based on a sample of 737 breakaway gaps from 132 stocks. Bearish breakaway gaps (bull market, downward breakout from a congestion region) take an average of 168 days to fill the gap.

- Breakaway gaps appear as price leaves a consolidation region on high volume. The gap does not close quickly.

Figure 5.8 shows an example of a breakaway gap when price leaves the congestion area.

Continuation Gaps Continuation gaps are rare. I found 495 of them, but it took 173 stocks. They appear most often in a straight-line run higher, usually sandwiched between a breakaway gap at the start and an exhaustion gap at the end. Thus, they appear midway along the price trend, so some call them measuring or runaway gaps. If you measure the height from the start of the trend to the middle of the continuation gap and project the result higher, you can gauge how far price is likely to climb.

The figure shows the measure rule for continuation gaps. Compute the distance from A to B (the gap center or the bottom of the gap, if you want to be more conservative) and add it to B to get the target, C.

Continuation gaps take an average of 98 days to close for upward breakouts and 77 days for downward breakouts. The gap appears in the price trend 43 and 57 percent of the way to the trend end for up and down trends, respectively.

* Continuation gaps appear near the middle of a straight-line run, often on high volume.

Exhaustion Gaps Exhaustion gaps occur near the end of trends. Often, a breakaway gap will send price shooting higher and an exhaustion gap completes the trend. Volume is high as traders scramble for the exits as if the building were on fire.

After the exhaustion gap, price moves sideways and retraces a portion of the run, often closing the gap. In other words, price does not continue making new highs (upward price trend) or new lows (downward trend). Exhaustion gaps can be quite large, so if you see a gap several points tall, it is apt to be an exhaustion gap.

Figure 5.8 shows an exhaustion gap that leads to the consolidation region. I found 471 exhaustion gaps in 173 stocks, and they closed in an average of 9 days for upward trends and 14 days for downward trends.

* Exhaustion gaps appear at the end of trends, on high volume, and close quickly.

How to Trade Gaps Trading gaps revolves around the gap type. Here are some tips.

* If a gap leaves a congestion area then it is a **breakaway gap**. It usually means a strong move ahead, since breakaway gaps take so long to close.

- If a gap occurs within a congestion area, moving up, but the price high does not extend above the high of the congestion region, then it is probably an **area gap**. Ignore it. Wait for price to break free of the congestion area before taking a position.
- Volume will not be a key to these gaps except for an **area gap**. Volume tends to recede quickly after an area gap since price does not move far before retracing and closing the gap. For the other types, volume will tend to remain high for a few days.
- *After* a trend is underway, then expect an **exhaustion gap**. Continuation gaps are rare enough that they are not much of a worry except in thinly traded stocks. Price should enter a congestion area almost immediately if it is an exhaustion gap. If price continues trending, then it is a continuation gap.
- If it is an **exhaustion gap**, then look for a violent reversal. Figure 5.1 shows an example of this at gaps J and K. If you can detect an exhaustion gap, then trading in the opposite direction can be a profitable short-term play (to catch the retrace move).
- If price makes a huge gap, then it is an **exhaustion gap**. Price will stop trending and consolidate, retracing some of the prior move.

10. The Never Lose Pattern: The Inverted Dead-Cat Bounce

I have sold stock 15 times because of an inverted dead-cat bounce and made money on each trade. At other times, I have decided to hold on for the longer term to make even more money. The inverted dead-cat bounce is one of my favorite event patterns, and I discuss it again in *Swing and day Trading*, Chapter 5.

For now though, imagine that you own IBM. Before the market open, the company announces better than expected earnings and the stock gaps 15 percent higher. What do you do?

If you have been paying attention, the gap is likely an exhaustion gap. The gap might not close anytime soon, but the chance of at least a partial retrace is high. If I had a profit in the stock, I would sell and wait for price to drop back in two weeks. After that, if I still liked the stock, then I could always rebuy it.

If a stock gaps higher on news, then consider selling it. Holding on usually means price will retrace its gains (at least partially) and you may decide to sell later, but at a lower price.

Sometimes, though, holding on is the best choice for a position trade. If the news announcement suggests better times ahead, then the stock may continue climbing, just at a slower rate. However, it is difficult to gauge how the stock will respond.

For example, I thought Southwest Airlines stock would continue to do well in June 2004 when they reached a tentative contract with the flight attendants union. After the announcement, price rose only 8 percent, but it turned a small paper profit into a larger one. I decided to hold on, but the stock dropped like a jet fighter hit by an AMRAAM missile. A stop loss order parachuted me out of the stock with a 3 percent loss. That was the good news because the stock continued to decline 14 percent below where I sold.

- If the market hands you a gain, grab it and run to the bank.

DETERMINING STOCK OR MARKET DIRECTION

Determining market direction is more art than science. It is like telling you how to hit a tennis ball at a can I have placed on the far side of the court. I can tell you to aim a bit more to the right, but I cannot give you the skill to consistently knock the darn thing over. You have to develop that yourself. I can give you some useful tips, though, like *aim for the can, not the referee.* Tips 11 through 14 are useful for short-term traders.

11. What Are the Futures Doing?

If you have been trading long enough, then you probably know this tip: What are the S&P and Nasdaq futures doing? I use the Yahoo! Finance website because they show the futures versus fair value before the market open. If the value is a double-digit number like 20 or higher (or –20 and lower), then expect the market to open positive (negative).

- If the S&P or Nasdaq futures make a big move, either higher or lower, expect the stock market to open accordingly.

12. Price Jumps. Now What?

Figure 5.9 shows two candles. The one on the left is a pattern you may come across if price does an inverted dead-cat bounce. Recall that price shoots up on news in that event pattern. Often price will close at or near the day's high. The figure shows what typically happens the next day, and that is important if you want to sell.

I used 565 stocks from October 2005 to September 2010 and found 14,557 instances of stocks closing at the exact high of the day. Then I evaluated what happened the next day.

FIGURE 5.9 The right candle is the typical profile when price closes the prior day at the high.

Will price make a higher high? Yes, 81 percent of the time, but the stock will close lower 55 percent of the time. How much higher will the stock go that day? The median rise is 1.38 percent. Thus, you have a 50-50 chance of seeing your stock rise 1.38 percent above the prior day's close. One third of the stocks will climb over 2.5 percent higher.

If you feel the stock is going to drop the day after price closes at the high, then place a limit order to sell 1.38 percent above the prior high. Price should hit the target about half the time.

For reference, **Table 5.3** shows the frequency distribution of the distance above the prior close on a percentage basis. For example, 9 percent of the time, stocks climbed less than 0.25 percent above the prior close. Two thirds of the time (67 percent), stocks failed to post a high 2.25 percent above the prior close. Use the table to help determine the price at which to place a limit order.

- After price jumps higher and if it closes at the high for the day, place a limit order to sell the next day at 1.38 percent above the close. That should hit about half the time.

13. Chasing Tails for Profit

Many moons ago, I read that tails are more reliable when they appear at minor lows than at minor highs. That is true, and I will discuss my proof in a moment. First, what is a tail?

TABLE 5.3 Frequency Distribution of Price Rises

Distance	0.25%	0.50%	0.75%	1.00%	1.25%
Distribution	9%	11%	10%	9%	8%
Cumulative	9%	20%	30%	39%	47%

Distance	1.50%	1.75%	2.00%	2.25%	2.50%
Distribution	6%	6%	5%	4%	33%
Cumulative	53%	59%	63%	67%	100%

A *bearish tail,* or *spike* as they are sometimes called, is a one-day price line that towers above the surrounding countryside like a lone tree on a hill (for minor highs). The idea is that when a tall price bar closes near the day's low, it means the bulls tried to hold a new high but could not, so a down move will follow.

For *bullish tails,* the spikes point downward and drop far below the adjacent price action. They appear at valleys, and price must close near the day's high. They suggest that bears made a push lower during the day, but could not hold off the buying pressure that forced price to close above the low for the day. It suggests a rising price trend will come.

Figure 5.10 shows a few examples at minor highs (D and C) and minor lows (A and B). Using the rules for the test that follows, no other tails appear on the chart (often because of the location of the closing price).

Table 5.4 shows the results of a test I performed using 565 stocks from October 2000 to September 2010. I found all minor highs or lows that were at least 5 days from adjacent peaks or valleys (which is why point D qualifies in Figure 5.10). That means the peak holding the potential tail must be the highest high from 5 days before to 5 days after the peak (11 days total).

FIGURE 5.10   Tails at minor highs and lows.

TABLE 5.4 Results of Tails at Minor Highs and Lows

Description	Average Rise or Decline	5% Failure Rate
Tails at minor highs	−13%	11%
No tails at minor highs	−11%	17%
Tails at minor low	14%	8%
No tails at minor lows	13%	11%

The same applies to valleys, 5 days before to 5 days after the valley holding the lowest low.

Having found a peak or valley, I looked for price to overlap the two adjacent days no more than 50 percent. That filter left spikes that towered above/below the surrounding landscape. Then I qualified the remaining with a closing price that must be near (within half of the bar's height) the low (for minor highs) or near the high (for minor lows). Some require closer values, but a review of the selections showed the process was working.

I measured the drop from the highest high at the tail to the next valley's low, or the lowest low at the tail (for a minor low) to the high at the next peak. These are the swing lows and swing highs, and Table 5.4 shows the percentage moves.

For example, when a bearish tail appeared at a minor high, price dropped an average of 13 percent from peak to trough. When no tail appeared, the drop averaged just 11 percent.

For bullish tails, the rise from trough to peak averaged 14 percent compared to 13 percent for those minor lows not showing tails.

In both cases, tails signaled a slightly larger move.

To determine which type of tail (bullish or bearish) works better, a direct comparison of the average rise or decline is not a fair test. A stock can only lose all of its value (a drop of 100 percent), but the rise can be unlimited. I decided to count how many stocks failed to move less than 5 percent after the tail. The measure is the same as discussed for the prior test (meaning from the highest peak to next valley or lowest low to next peak).

I found that bearish tails—those at minor highs—had 11 percent failing to drop price more than 5 percent. That compares to an 8 percent failure rate for bullish tails. When no tails were involved, the failure rates were much higher, 17 and 11 percent, respectively.

Based on the numbers in Table 5.4, bullish tails are more reliable than bearish ones. This makes sense since the market favors bulls over bears (look at the Dow Jones Industrial average in the 1920s compared to where it is today).

- Bullish tails appear at minor lows as price spikes below the adjacent price bars, but close near the high. They signal a move higher.
- Bearish tails appear at minor highs like a lone tree on a hill. They mean a downturn is coming. They are not as reliable as bullish tails.

One note of caution: Do not try to trade tails and expect to make the gains shown in Table 5.4. The results are for hundreds of *perfect* swing trades.

14. Tall Price Bar Retrace

Have you ever wondered what price does the day after a large move? I decided to find out and used 565 stocks from October 2005 to September 2010, locating 21,656 samples. I looked for price bars that were more than twice as tall as the 22-trading day (about one calendar month) average. To determine the trend, I used linear regression over the prior nine calendar days of closing prices.

Table 5.5 shows the results. The table uses percentages of the up or down trend, respectively (the Ignore Trend column uses all samples).

For example, during an upward, short-term price trend, stocks made a higher high the day after a tall price bar 31 percent of the time. If price trended down, they made a new high 32 percent of the time. If you ignore the inbound trend, price made a new high 32 percent of the time after a tall price bar. To flip that around, it means price failed to make a new high 68 percent of the time (it retraced).

The next row in the table shows how often price made a lower low after a tall price bar as a percentage of up or down trends, respectively. The results are similar to the prior row with price making a lower low most often when the trend is upward. That is a countertrend move.

- Price fails to make a lower low (downward price trends) or higher high (upward trends) the day after a tall price bar at least 68 percent of the time.

TABLE 5.5 Price Behavior after a Tall Price Bar

	Trend Up	Trend Down	Ignore Trend
Higher high	31%	32%	32%
Lower low	28%	27%	27%
Higher close	48%	47%	48%
Lower close	51%	52%	51%

The bottom two rows in Table 5.5 show where price *closes* the day after a tall price bar when compared to the prior close. Most often (51 or 52 percent), price will close lower regardless of the upward or downward trend.

- After a tall price bar, price shows a slight tendency to close lower the next day.

FINDING THE MARKET BOTTOM

How many times have you gone bottom fishing for stocks and after buying, found out that it was not the bottom after all? I suffered through that right along with everyone else during the 2007 to 2009 bear market. However, I cut my position size to as much as one-eighth of what is was at the bull market peak and then tested the waters when I felt I could make some money. Eventually, the market turned and I started piling in, catching the turn within days for some of my utility stocks.

How did I catch the market bottom? Tips 15 through 20 discuss that.

15. Ugly Double Bottom: A Higher Bottom

A higher bottom is what I lovingly call an ugly double bottom. That is when price forms a second bottom that is at least 5 percent higher than the first one. It becomes an ugly double bottom when price *closes* above the peak between those two bottoms.

For example, the March trend down in Figure 5.10 shows major turning points in which the second bottom is lower than the first. Only at point A do we see the first hint of a trend change. Point A is not at least 5 percent higher than the prior bottom, so it does not qualify as an ugly double bottom.

Consider the downtrend in Figure 5.7. At C and D, price forms two bottoms, but D is only 3 percent higher than C, so it does not qualify as an ugly double bottom. Ignore it. It is not an investment quality pattern.

Now look at bottoms A and B. Those two valleys are over 17 percent apart. When price closes above the peak between A and B, the squiggles become a valid ugly double bottom. A buy stop placed a penny above the high would get you in a rising price trend that climbed 25 percent until peaking in January 2009.

Here are the guidelines for identifying ugly double bottoms.

- Price trends downward leading to the first bottom.
- Two valleys bottom, but the second is at least 5 percent higher than the first.
- Volume recedes 81 percent of the time from bottom to bottom.

- The pattern becomes valid when price *closes* above the peak between the two bottoms.

Waiting for an ugly double bottom to confirm as valid will reduce your bottom fishing losses. Think I am kidding? Check any chart with a downward price trend and see how often the pattern signals a profitable turn. The key is to wait for confirmation. If the pattern does not confirm, then price will continue lower. If it *does* confirm, then you have a good chance at making money, and you may be buying near the bottom.

16. Bullish Chart Patterns Appear

When price makes new highs for the year, bullish chart patterns head south for the winter. For example, a double *bottom* is *unlikely* to appear when price makes new highs. Instead, you see double tops, head-and-shoulder tops, and other types of *bearish* patterns, not bullish ones.

At market bottoms, however, bullish patterns stick their noses out of the hole like a rabbit sniffing the air. This is especially true of pipe bottoms. I do not know what it is about pipes, but they are as plentiful as night crawlers after a rainstorm.

Switch to the weekly scale. Look for two price spikes adjacent to one another and poking well below the surrounding terrain. The two spikes need not be the same length. In fact, performance improves if they are different lengths, but that is in a bull market. In a bear market when the stock bottoms near the same price, performance improves. Figure 5.7 shows a pipe bottom at B.

What I have seen is many pipe bottoms appear in the same industry and in other stocks as the market bottoms. When that happens, it is not the absolute bottom. Rather, price bounces and then forms a second bottom. Pipes appear again at the second bottom, too, just not as many as the first time. That second bottom could be the turning point between bear and bull market.

- When many stocks show pipe bottoms, look for a bounce leading to a second bottom. That second bottom may spell the end of the bear market.

17. Stock Downgrades Plentiful

When brokers downgrade stocks, the bottom is near. I did an analysis of rating downgrades on the stocks I follow from January 1995 to September 2010. **Table 5.6** shows the results for the two bear markets, March 2000 to October 2002 and October 2007 to March 2009.

I used 745 stocks and found 8,984 rating changes. I logged the date of the change and the price of the S&P 500 index on that date, not the price of

TABLE 5.6 Stock Rating Changes Over Time

Market	Type	0–25% Bear Market Start	26–50%	51–75%	76–100% Bear Market End
2000–2002 Bear	Upgrades	17%	28%	27%	28%
2000–2002 Bear	Downgrades	16%	38%	16%	31%
2007–2009 Bear	Upgrades	31%	20%	28%	21%
2007–2009 Bear	Downgrades	22%	22%	22%	34%

the stock. This method allowed tracking of the rating change compared to the market environment.

The idea behind this method is that since a rising tide lifts all boats, determining when that tide is about to come in or go out is useful. The tide is a metaphor for the general market.

Let us go through each of the four rows in the table. The percentages across the top of the table show where in the bear market the rating change took place, both on a time and price basis (which happened to show the same results), when compared to the S&P 500 index.

For the 2000 to 2002 bear market, encouraging investors to buy stocks with a rating upgrade just as the market turns bearish is an unlucky call. Fortunately, that only happened 17 percent of the time. At the right end of the table, only 28 percent of the stocks had rating *upgrades* within 25 percent of the *end* of the bear market. Just as the market was about to bottom, few brokers were making bullish calls.

For downgrades, just 16 percent of the stocks within 25 percent of the start of a bear market warned of a coming decline. That means 84 percent were still bullish. Fully 31 percent suggested more problems ahead just as the bear market was ending.

For the 2007 to 2009 bear market, 31 percent of the stocks had upgrades just as the bear market began. Oops! Twenty-one percent posted upgrades near the end of the bear market. Rating downgrades were flat at 22 percent until near the end of the bear market where downgrades spiked, to 34 percent. Brokers downgraded stocks just before they were about to rally.

- When brokers downgrade stocks across the board and upgrade few, the end of the bear market could be near.
- When many brokers upgrade stocks and few downgrade, a bear market could be approaching.

18. You Feel Like Selling Everything

Buy-and-hold investors that look at their portfolios frequently in a bear market find their emotions tweaked. As the bear shreds their holdings like beef found at a campsite, investors become more and more disgusted with the dwindling value.

Eventually, they fear that the market is going to zero, and that they should move their holdings to cash. When everyone else makes the same decision, volume increases, price spikes down (or makes a straight-line move down over a few days) and then a recovery begins. That is the end of the bear market.

Of course, in the moment, it is difficult to tell when that happens. Perhaps numbers can provide some guidance. The bear market began in March 2000 at a peak of 1552.87 in the S&P and bottomed in October 2002 at 768.63 for a decline of 51 percent. The 2007 to 2009 bear market tumbled 58 percent. In other words, if you feel like selling everything, compute the decline in the S&P 500 index from the high to the current value. If it is down about 50 percent, then you are near the bottom. You might as well hold on. The 1972 to 1973 bear market dropped price 50 percent.

- If the S&P 500 index is down 50 percent from the high, it is near bottom.

19. High Volume Bottom

In the scenario just described, where people look at the value of their portfolios and decide to sell, volume spikes upward. These climax bottoms are difficult to spot because of irregular shaped volume on the indices.

If you flip to the monthly price scale and look at volume during the last two bear markets, you will see that volume peaked during the month in which price bottomed. In October 1987, another bearish month, volume peaked and the index declined 34 percent.

Compare that to the October 1, 1974, bear market bottom. Volume spiked, making it the second highest peak for that year.

- Volume spikes at bear market bottoms.

20. Bad News Moves Nothing, Good News Lifts Market

This is my favorite indicator for detecting a major market bottom. When bad news does not cause the market to make a huge drop, and good news sends it soaring, then you have found your bottom, or at least a bullish retrace in a bear market.

To gauge this, I search the news, especially when it makes a large move (more than 150 points). Why did the market index go up? If unemployment claims skyrocket and the market drops 30 points (yawn), then that is a good sign. Bad unemployment reports can send the markets tumbling hundreds of points, but when they do not, then that is a clue of a market turn.

Do not let one economic report send you and your shopping cart scurrying for the nearest cash register with the shortest line. Often the authorities revise economic reports. However, when the preponderance of evidence shows that bad news is no longer hurting the market like it used to, and good news is lifting it off the bottom, then that could signal a market bottom.

- When good news lifts the market and bad news has little effect, expect the end of a bear market. When the reverse is true, expect a market decline.

21. Getting in Early: Partial Rises and Declines

Figure 5.11 shows an example of what I call a partial decline. This one occurs in a broadening bottom chart pattern. A broadening pattern is just as it sounds.

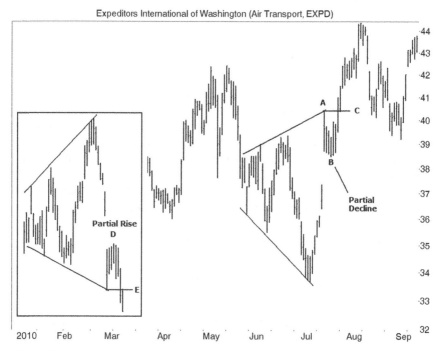

FIGURE 5.11   A partial decline in a broadening bottom chart pattern suggests an upward breakout.

Price makes higher peaks and lower valleys over time. Each side should have at least two touches of the respective trendline (but three or more is best).

Once a valid pattern is established, meaning enough trendline touches have occurred, then look for price to touch the top trendline and move lower, but not come that close to the bottom trendline before reversing. When it again touches the top trendline, price often stages an immediate upward breakout. That is a partial decline.

Figure 5.11 shows an example where price touches each broadening bottom trendline three times with the last touch at A. After that, price drops to B, and then curls around before breaking out of the chart pattern at C. C represents a line drawn horizontally at the top of the chart pattern. A close above that price means an upward breakout. A partial decline occurs at B when price leaves the top trendline and then reverses direction to break out upward.

Imagine that the broadening bottom is flipped upside down, which I show in the inset. Point D represents a partial rise. It behaves the same way as a partial decline, only inverted. Price touches the bottom trendline, moves up to D—not touching or coming that close to the top trendline, and then drops, staging a breakout when price closes below E.

In searching for examples to use for Figure 5.11, I came to the conclusion that partial rises and declines do not work as well as they used to. From 1991 to 2004, partial declines in broadening bottoms correctly predicted an upward breakout in a bull market 80 percent of the time. In broadening tops, a partial rise worked 72 percent of the time in a bull market. I have not tested more recent patterns to see how the technique behaves, so be cautious using this method.

Partial declines and partial rises occur most often in the various types of broadening patterns and rectangles.

- A partial rise predicts a downward breakout. A partial decline predicts an upward breakout.

22. Pattern Width and Performance

I read in a magazine that wide patterns take longer for price to reach their targets than narrow ones. It said that common practice was to hold for one pattern width, but they found that the longer you hold, the better you tend to do. They recommend holding for three times the pattern width.

I decided to run my own test. I used 45 different types of chart patterns in 1,283 stocks from May 1988 to July 2010 and found 26,873 known good patterns (meaning I inspected each one, over the years, and that they are not a product of automated pattern recognition).

I measured the width of each chart pattern from start to end and then found where the ultimate high or low represented a trend change (a decline or rise of at least 20 percent, respectively). The performance numbers shown in **Table 5.7** represent thousands of *perfect* trades, so your results may vary.

The table shows a frequency distribution of the associated rise or decline from the closing price the day before a breakout (to allow for gaps) to the ultimate high (upward breakouts) or low (downward breakouts).

For example, chart patterns with upward breakouts tended to rise to the ultimate high quickly. In fact, 38 percent found it within one pattern width and 20 percent topped out within two pattern widths. I found that 69 percent of chart patterns with upward breakouts peaked within three pattern widths (that is the sum of 38, 20, and 11 percent).

The next line down in the table shows performance sorted by the time it took to reach the ultimate high as a multiple of the pattern's width. Those that find the ultimate high within one pattern width climbed an average of 18 percent. Patterns that took between one and two pattern widths soared 29 percent on average. After three pattern widths, the rate of rise tends to flatten, at least for a while.

That is especially true for downward breakouts, which tend to poop out after widths of two (they decline an average of 24 percent). For example, patterns that take four pattern widths to reach the ultimate low decline an average of 27 percent below the close the day before the breakout. That is the same for five pattern widths, too. The numbers suggest that holding for longer than two pattern widths gives little extra return for the risk involved.

Notice the difference in performance between upward and downward breakouts. Patterns with upward breakouts that take eight multiples of the pattern width perform twice as well as those with downward breakouts. The reason for that is because a stock can have unlimited gains, but can only lose 100 percent of its value.

- After an upward breakout from a chart pattern, holding a stock for up to three pattern widths tends to see the best gains in the shortest time.

TABLE 5.7 Frequency Distribution of Pattern Width versus Performance

Width Multiplier:	1	2	3	4	5	6	7	8	9	>9
Distribution	38%	20%	11%	7%	5%	4%	3%	2%	1%	9%
Gain	18%	29%	37%	43%	44%	47%	54%	56%	65%	72%
Up Breakouts (Above)				**Down breakouts (Below)**					
Distribution	55%	21%	10%	5%	3%	2%	1%	1%	1%	2%
Loss	17%	24%	25%	27%	27%	28%	30%	28%	32%	31%

• After a downward breakout from a chart pattern, shorting the stock for longer than two pattern widths gives little extra return for the risk involved.

23. Price Drops Faster than It Rises

"Price drops faster than it rises," Linda told me during a phone call. How did she know? "Experience," she said. Many people suspect that it is true, but how do you prove it? I found a way and documented the numbers in my *Encyclopedia of Chart Patterns* book.

I like to use symmetrical triangles since they break out upward 56 percent of the time (using numbers updated to mid-2011), meaning the direction is nearly random. In a bull market, price gains an average of 29 percent in 139 days compared to downward breakouts that drop 13 percent in 43 days. I rest my case.

"Huh?" you may ask. If price drops 13 percent in 43 days that means it should rise 40 percent in 139 days if the two velocities were the same. If you still do not get it, change the days to 40 and 120. If the upward breakout takes three times as long, it should rise three times as far, or 39 percent (13 percent × 3) instead of the 29 percent that it actually does. The drop is much faster than the rise.

• Price drops faster than it rises.

This not only applies to symmetrical triangles, but other chart patterns as well. Chart patterns just provide a convenient vehicle to test such behavior. The implication of this is significant. You can make more money shorting a stock than buying long. It also means that if price breaks out downward from a chart pattern when you expected an upward breakout, then sell immediately. Often the first few days after a breakout tend to see the largest moves, so reaction speed is important.

24. Mirrors for Trend Prediction

How many of you cannot resist looking at yourself in the mirror when you pass by one? As you look at yourself, consider the symmetry. You have one shoulder on the left and one on the right, just as you do eyes, ears, and even nostrils.

Price patterns sometimes have the same type of symmetry, and that can help you determine where price is going. A head-and-shoulders top relies on symmetry in both price and time. Each shoulder should peak near the same price and be similar distances from the head.

Consider **Figure 5.12**. The chart reminds me of my college days. I was hoping to get a four-year scholarship to pay for college by joining the

FIGURE 5.12 Peaks and valleys appear near the same distance from the center line.

Air Force as a pilot. One of the tests they administer shows two aerial views of terrain (like a city) with a dozen or more points highlighted (to make it more difficult, one chart has more points identified than the other). Your task is to match one point on the left picture with the proper one on the right.

It may sound easy, but you have to do it in 30 seconds and the two figures are taken at different focal lengths (one is zoomed, but not the other), at different times of the day, and rotated. I do not think I answered any of the questions right. Decades later, I am a leading expert on pattern recognition. Go figure! As you might have guessed, they did not give me a scholarship. Apparently, knowing how to navigate is important to pilots....

Anyway, returning to Figure 5.12, notice how the points to the left of the vertical line match those on the right. If you were to blank out the right half, you could take the left half, flip it over, and use that as a proxy to navigate the price terrain as it unfolded.

For example, points A and B approximate the same height and distance from the line. C and D match up as do E and F. Look at the decline from A to G. Notice how it matches the rise from G to B.

These types of price mirrors work surprisingly well. They are not very effective in a rising price trend (such as when price breaks out to a new high).

It will not be perfect as the chart shows, but at least it gives you a clue of what to expect.

* Think of what price will do in the future by reflecting price movement around a peak or valley.

25. Trendline Mirrors: Another Reflection

How many times have you asked yourself how far price was going to drop after a trendline break? Trendline mirrors give you an answer. Consider trendline AB in **Figure 5.13**. Since price is trending upward, I drew the line along the valleys.

Price signaled that it was moving lower when it pierced the trendline in February. I measured the distance from the prior peak to the trendline, C to D: 33.35 – 28.90 or 4.45. Reflecting this rise across the trendline where price finally decided to make its move lower (E at 30.21), gives a target of 30.21 – 4.45 or 25.76. Price at F bottoms at 25.89, missing the target by just 13 cents.

Will this technique work all of the time? No. Price sometimes pierces a trendline and hugs it before trending at a shallower angle. That is especially

FIGURE 5.13 A trendline mirror from C to D matches the distance from E to F.

true when price pierces a steep trendline. I also used the log scale for price. That effects where the trendline intersects price, so if you use the linear scale, you will have different results.

- Reflect the vertical distance across a trendline to help predict how far price will drop.

This reflection technique also works for down-sloping trendlines. However, the projection might serve as a minimum move since upward moves tend to travel further.

26. Avoid Price Mountains

A price mountain is just as it sounds: Price makes a big move up and then slides back down. **Figure 5.14** shows an example.

Before I discuss price mountains, notice that A and C mirror B and D around peak E. In other words, the points on the left of the peak also appear on the right. It is another example of a price mirror, but this time the chart is on the monthly scale.

FIGURE 5.14 A price mountain appears and, a decade later, the stock still has not recovered.

The figure shows Intel during the tech bubble at the turn of the millennium, and the stock chart is representative of other tech issues from that era. The price scale is linear to emphasize the stock's rise and fall.

Notice that a decade later, price still has not recovered or even come close to the old peak. Those investors who bought the stock on the climb to the summit at E have had to wait over a decade to make their money back, and they are still waiting.

The moral of this story is simple. If a stock forms a price mountain, do not expect price to recover anytime soon.

Let us look at this differently. Imagine that the bear market of 2000 to 2002 has ended and price has been climbing up the chart to point F. A series of tall white candles speak of enthusiasm that traders probably felt as price climbed up the mountain from C to E. Can we expect the uptrend to continue?

It reached 74 before, why not again? The answer is that another bubble will come along, but it probably will not be in semiconductor stocks. For example, biotech stocks are hot now. If a new drug gets approved by the FDA, price can climb as fast as the heartbeat in a patient with a blood pressure problem. The chart of Human Genome Sciences (HGSI) shows the same pattern as Intel except for a flatter aftermath. Price peaked near 116 in 2000, and has made it as high as 35 a decade later and is at 14.24 now (August 2012).

- Avoid investing in stocks showing a price mountain.

How Long to Summit a Price Mountain?   Figure 5.14 and the above text make it sound like decades will pass before price again tries to summit a price mountain, so I researched how long it takes.

I programmed my computer to find all peaks after which price declined by at least 50 percent, from January 1990 to September 2010. I combed through 565 stocks, giving me 481 samples. Each stock had to maintain a closing price above $3. This eliminated securities I did not want included because stock splits can reduce historical prices to mere pennies. Small movements in those stocks represent unrealistic percentage changes.

It took an average of 4.3 years for price to exceed a price mountain. If you include those mountains that have not been exceeded yet, the average time climbs to 4.9 years. If you only tally those not rising to the old peak yet, the average climbs to 5.6 years, and counting.

- On average, it can take more than five years for price to recover after a price mountain.

Fourteen Selling Tips You Need to Know

Determining when to sell and actually selling can be easy or difficult, depending on how you manage your money. One useful technique for a long holding is to ask if now is the time to go short? If a holding has been bleeding money, seeming to drop almost every day with no end in sight, is it time to close out the position? If you can ignore that you own the stock and look at it as a prospective short candidate, then that may help.

One of my favorite techniques is to switch positions with my mom. If she owned the stock and I did not, what would I tell her to do with it? Then I follow the advice.

- When contemplating a trading decision, what would you tell your parents to do with the same stock?

The selling decision is a mental game. Every small loss becomes a large one a dollar at a time. Not cutting your losses short means they will grow. When was the last time a huge loser actually recovered to show a profit? Did it take years? Look back at Figure 5.14 and ask yourself how long do the people that bought Intel above 40 have to hold the stock just to break even?

If you want to learn how to sell, then I recommend the book, *When to Sell* (Mamis 1977), but the following tips may also help. These 14 tips, numbered 27 through 40 in my list, help you determine when to sell.

27. Use stops.
28. Sell when wrong.
29. Sell on the unexpected.
30. Sell on trend change.
31. Sell blue chips on 10 percent down.
32. Indicator says sell: Obey it.
33. Follow your rules.
34. Sell on confirmation of bearish pattern.
35. Sell at price target.
36. Sell on piercing support.
37. Sell on industry weakness.
38. Weak fundamentals.
39. Sell on hype.
40. What would Tom do?

27. Use Stops

I have already discussed stops, so this deserves only a brief mention now. Instead of agonizing over whether to sell a stock, using a properly placed stop loss order removes the anxiety that occurs during a sell decision. You do not have to monitor the stock's every move like a day trader. Instead, the stop does the work and takes you out when things go wrong.

Let me put it another way. The professionals use stops; they know when to sell. Are you taking your trading seriously or are you just playing? Turn into a pro by using properly placed stops.

• Use stop loss orders for short-term trades.

28. Sell When Wrong

Before making an investment, ask yourself how far is price likely to move, both up and down? At what price will the market be saying I made a mistake? Framing the questions like that *before* trading can pinpoint the exit price. Knowing when to quit and walk away from the game is half the battle. Complete the other half by placing a stop at the designated exit price.

• At what price will the market tell me I am making a mistake?

29. Sell on the Unexpected

Sometimes I buy into a chart pattern before it confirms, like a double bottom with a shelf on the right bottom. A shelf occurs when price moves horizontally for several days, forming a flat top. It is a support area and a good place to buy. A stop placed below the shelf keeps the potential loss tiny while the double bottom predicts a large upward move.

Unfortunately, that setup does not work every time. Sometimes the stock catches cold and drops. If the stop is there, then it will catch the bearish change. If not, then I sell when the unexpected happens. I expected the stock to go up but it did not. Exit time.

Here is another example. Symmetrical triangles are notorious for double busting, as I mentioned. If price breaks out in my favor and then collapses to breakout in the opposite direction, I close out the trade. It might double bust, or it could drop in half, but I am not sticking around to find out. I exit the trade. Stat!

Another situation occurs when bottom fishing. Price has been trending lower for months, so it must be close to bottoming. "If it was a good deal at 50, it's a steal at 25," your broker says. "It's a 50 percent off sale! What's not to like?"

You buy the stock at 25 only to discover what owning it at 10 feels like. Clearly, the stock is closer to bottoming now than before, but zero is still far below. It could drop that far. If the original purchase is a mistake, then exit the trade immediately.

- If a stock makes an adverse or unexpected move, sell it.

30. Sell on Trend Change

If the market drops 20 percent from a peak, we classify that as a bear market. A bull market is one that rises by 20 percent from a valley. Why not apply that designation to individual stocks? I classify a 20 percent reversal as a trend change.

If a stock is down 20 percent or more from a high, then it has moved into bear territory. Dump it. This simple rule will limit most losses to 20 percent (but a stock can gap down, leaving you with a 60 percent hole in your wallet). That is still huge, but it is better than seeing your favorite stock turn into a mediocre play, and then into a dog when it eases lower day by day until it is threatening bankruptcy. Do not let that happen. Sell after a trend change occurs.

- If a stock drops 20 percent from a high, sell it.

31. Sell Blue Chips 10 Percent Down

One money manager I know uses 10 percent as the sell threshold, but only on blue chip stocks. With the other stocks, she gives them more room to fluctuate. "Deciding when to sell a long-term holding is tough," she says.

Here is how she does it. When a blue chip stock drops 5 percent from a peak, she takes a closer look. The drop is a warning that something could be changing either on the fundamental or technical side.

When price drops 10 percent, then the warning light has changed to a sell signal. She sells at least half, but often the entire position. This only applies to blue chip stocks, those that do not fluctuate much from day to day.

For non-blue chips, it is better to use other methods.

- Sell a blue chip when it drops 10 percent from a peak.

32. Indicator Says Sell: Obey It

I am not an indicator person. That means my favorite indicator is price, not volume, not RSI, nor CCI, nor any other pneumonic for an indicator. You may be different. Perhaps you like MACD. Fine. But when it says sell, then sell. Go ahead and look for other confirming information that supports your decision.

If you confirm the indicator sell signal with other indicators, then make sure they add value. I remember reading of someone using MACD with a moving average crossover scheme. Why? Both techniques use moving averages, so he was depending on a duplicated signal.

If you use three indicators and all of them are momentum based, then that is not the diversity you seek.

- Are you selling based on a trend following indicator when price is moving in a trading range?
- Are you using an indicator built for trading ranges when price is trending?
- Do you use too many indicators that do not add value?

Have faith in the tools you use, but select the proper one for the job. In a pinch, a chisel will work as a screwdriver, but do you really want to turn that screw with a finely honed chisel?

If you open your toolbox and see three flat head screwdrivers of the same size, do you need two of them? Keep only the indicators that work best. That way, when you get a sell signal, you can sell with confidence.

Try this experiment. Plot and overlay your indicators on the same chart as price. If they are all turning at the same time, then what do you need them for? You can just look at price and determine how your indicators are signaling. Keep it simple.

- Overlay your indicators on the same price chart to see if they signal at the same time. Remove duplicates.
- Understand your indicators so that when they say sell, you believe them.

33. Follow Your Rules

Look back at your trades and ask yourself this question: If I had followed my rules, would I have made more money? Answering that question provides a simple but powerful tool.

I told this story to my brother to make a point about selling. Joe owned IBM at $50 a share with a stop loss order at 47. The stock dropped to 47.25 and he removed the stop because he was convinced that the stock would recover and did not want to be stopped out before the big move. What happened?

The stock dropped to 46.39 the next day. Then a miracle occurred. The stock started a determined run, posting gains each day for three weeks. He sold the stock at 62 and change.

Several trades later, Widget Inc. eased lower, almost day by day. Joe had a stop on it at 23. When the stock approached that price, he again removed the stop. "It worked before," he said. "It will work again."

The stock continued lower for a few days, but then bounced. The recovery was not as steep as IBM, but by holding, he sold for a handsome profit. It seemed that Joe had a knack for knowing when the stock would bottom.

On the next trade, he does not even bother placing a stop, but has a mental turning point of 10.50. "If the stock drops below that, then it is time to sell."

Each day, the stock eased lower. Then it got clobbered, dropping from 10.63 to 9.75 in one session, a plunge of 8 percent. "It's only 88 cents," he said. "It'll turn soon." He was an expert at calling the bottoms, so he knew the turn was near. All he had to do was ride it out for the big bounce that would surely follow.

This time, though, the close below 10 pierced a major support level, but as a novice, Joe did not know about such things. The 8 percent drop was just the beginning of a quick move down that saw the stock tumble each day. Soon, the stock hit 6.63.

A month later, the stock bottomed at 4.27. Did it triple overnight to bring it back to breakeven at 13? No. Instead, the stock stayed flat for over a year.

What did Joe do wrong? He broke his rule (removing a stop) and got lucky when IBM recovered. That move created a bad habit, reinforced by success with Widgets. That set him up for a portfolio-draining loss in the last trade.

- If you followed your trading rules, would you make more money?

34. Sell on Confirmation of Bearish Pattern

What does *confirmation* mean? It varies from chart pattern to pattern, but it often means that price closes outside a trendline boundary or moves beyond the height of the chart pattern (that is, price closes above the top or below the bottom of a chart pattern). A confirmed pattern changes the random price squiggles into a valid buy or sell signal.

I have sold stocks before confirmation of a bearish chart pattern and saved money when price dropped. I have also sold too early and watched as price reversed, leaving me drooling on the sidelines when the stock became a moon shot.

An example of this would be selling during formation of the right shoulder of a head-and-shoulders top. Price drops, but does not close below the neckline (the confirmation signal), before price recovers.

If price *does* confirm a bearish chart pattern, then sell, and do it quickly. As I have explained, price drops faster than it rises. Selling as soon as you discover your mistake can save you millions (dream big).

- Sell if a bearish chart pattern confirms as valid.

35. Sell at Price Target

There is an old joke that says shoot first and then claim that whatever you hit was the target. For short-term traders (swing and day traders), sell when price reaches a predetermined target.

I use the chart pattern measure rule to set a target. For many chart patterns, take the height of the pattern and add it to the breakout price to get the target.

For example, if the height of an Eve & Eve double bottom, from the lowest bottom to the peak between the two bottoms, is $5 and the breakout price is $100, then the target becomes $105. Price will reach the target 67 percent of the time in a bull market if it behaves like the 412 patterns I studied in my *Encyclopedia of Chart Patterns* book.

Here is another tip. If you multiply the height by the percentage meeting the price target, you will get a closer, more reliable target. In this case, the new target would be $100 + $5 × 67 percent or $103.35.

- Use the measure rule for chart patterns to gauge how far price is likely to move. Multiply the pattern's height by the percentage meeting the price target (found in *Encyclopedia of Chart Patterns*) to get a more reliable target.

When using the measure rule, common sense must prevail. For example, if a stock closed at $10 and a double top has a height of $11, the measure rule says that price will decline below zero. Likewise, if an ascending triangle is $5 tall and the stock is priced at $10, will price really hit $15? That is a 50 percent rise! It is possible but unlikely.

- Convert the predicted rise or decline into a percentage to see if the move makes sense.

36. Sell on Piercing Support

The prior chapter discussed support and resistance, so you should be an expert on the subject. But how do you use it for trading?

If I find a support zone, I get alarmed when price *closes* below the region. I emphasize *closes* because a pierce will not do it. Many times, price will be like a tornado touching the ground and then climbing back into the clouds, never seen again. If price is going to drop, I want to be sure it is going down by waiting for a close below the bottom of the consolidation region.

For a quality support zone, I am looking for a solid block of horizontal price movement—the tighter the better. A loose structure has price with no determined direction, bobbing up and down like a cork on a pond during a storm.

Tight means lots of price overlap from day to day. It often appears as a solid black wall on the price chart. Then I determine how far away it is from the current price. If it is close by, say a few percentage points, it is possible that price will pierce that on the breakout and continue lower. If it is 4 to 12 percent away, then that makes it more likely that the stock will bounce off that support layer and pull back to the breakout price, giving me a second opportunity to cash out. I will discuss throwbacks and pullbacks below, but the point is to determine how far price is going to move and make a trading decision based on that.

- If price closes below support, then determine where price might stop declining. If support is nearby, then expect a pullback.

37. Sell on Industry Weakness

How many times has a stock in your portfolio cut the legs off a sister stock just because it is in the same industry? If other stocks in the industry begin to show weakness, then maybe it is time to sell.

Weakness can mean a trend change from up to down, or industry stocks can show bearish chart patterns like double tops and head-and-shoulders tops. Often, you will see the same chart pattern repeated in other industry stocks, perhaps with slight variations (the second top of a double top is lower than the prior one, for example, whereas in your stock, the double top looks perfect).

- Watch the behavior of stocks in the same industry as a clue to weakness or strength.

38. Weak Fundamentals

Fundamentals are a great tool for selecting undervalued quality stocks, but they are less useful in deciding when to sell. Why? Because the numbers you find in the quarterly report are at least one month old, perhaps more. I would rather depend on insider selling, but that is not much better. An insider can have many reasons to sell, but only buys the stock if he thinks it has potential.

Nevertheless, if you review the 10-Q or 10-K and find debt levels becoming excessive, cash flow drying up like a pond in summer, or sales plunging like a skydiver, then it is time to consider selling. That is especially true if product pricing is dropping due to competition or if raw material costs explode. That often happens in chemical firms.

Rising inventories in apparel retailers is another cause for concern. If no one is buying the merchandise, then they will have to mark it down until it sells.

I remember a trade in Hot Topic. I thought it was going to be another Michaels Stores, where I made almost 5,000 percent. It had the same features that I found appealing in Michaels. I studied the company. I asked my brother about it, and his girls loved the store. So, I bought the stock.

Then I learned that it was selling Goth merchandise. There is nothing wrong with the latest fashion trend, but it made me realize that the company was too trendy for my taste. I suspected that they would miss the next fashion turn, and I would be left holding the bag. I sold the stock for an 8 percent loss. Four days after I sold, the stock gapped 28 percent lower on disappointing store sales. Within a month, it had dropped another 31 percent. Wow. Fortunately, I took my small loss on a small position and ran out the door.

The price of oil is another fundamental worth tracking. A dropping price of oil benefits many industries and a rising price of jet fuel crashes airlines that do not hedge their costs (or guess wrongly). Other commodities play an important factor, too. Determine what are the key ingredients to a company's product and check whether their cost is increasing or decreasing. Sometimes this is spelled out in the quarterly report or 10-K, but you can also ask shareholder services.

- If the cost of goods sold is increasing at an usually high rate, it could be time to sell.
- Look for deteriorating fundamentals, such as overhead increasing faster than sales or profits.

39. Sell on Hype

If you own stock in a firm that makes pet rocks and you hear the late-night talk show hosts joking about pet rocks, then the time to cash out is approaching.

When hype becomes extreme and the stock is shooting skyward, then follow it closely or just sell. Waiting too long can be costly, especially if the stock decides to jump out the window and drop 70 percent overnight.

A good example of selling on hype occurs when you own a biotechnology stock and are waiting for FDA approval of a new drug. When that approval comes, consider selling at least half. Everyone wants to buy in, and that is the time you should be selling.

- Sell on hype. When everyone is talking about the latest gizmo, then the peak is near. Sell.

40. What Would Tom Do?

A financial consultant calls me for advice every few weeks. What I enjoy about her phone calls is that they reinforce my own beliefs. She will describe a trade and always sells if something changes. If the stock drops, she sells. If sales are weak, she visits nearby stores to get a better sense of the retail climate.

When I am struggling with a sell or hold decision, I ask this question: What would she do?

You can use me as a proxy. I am a market professional, a person who checks his emotion at the door when trading. If I owned your stock, would I sell it, buy more, or just hold on? Ask yourself, "What would Tom do?" Then act accordingly. This advice may sound stupid, but it works.

- When contemplating a sale, ask, "What would Tom do?"

VISUAL TIPS

The following five tips complete the chapter. These tips are visual ones that will help you decide when to take action and when not to. They help predict future price behavior, including my favorite, the triangle apex turn.

41. Drawing Three-Point Channels

Drawing three-point channels is a technique that is not well known, I think, but it has its uses. I show two methods for drawing them in **Figure 5.15.**

Imagine that you have three major turning points, such as those shown at A, B, and C. Draw a trendline connecting valleys A and C and extend that into the future (D). Draw a line parallel to the AC line starting at B. Notice that price reverses near E, which is near the top channel line. The lines extending from ABC form a three-point channel.

Draw three-point channels after a downward price trend to give you an idea of how price may move in the future. Unfortunately, it does not work very well. The technique depends on the slope of the AC line and how far price has climbed above that line, to B.

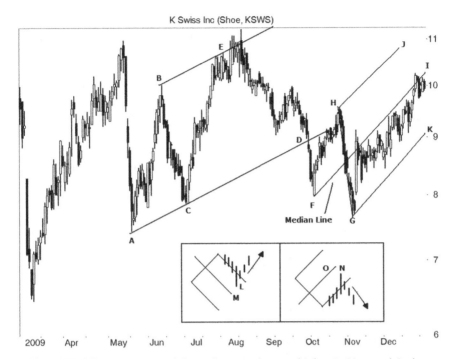

FIGURE 5.15 A three-point channel points the way higher in May, and Andrews pitchfork forms a channel in November.

If the slope is 30 to 45 degrees, then the line may hug price well (or at least follow it upward). Price seems to climb at about that angle. Lines steeper than that are probably too optimistic to be real.

If the stock does not hug the top trendline at E, then redraw the line so that it does. The parallel lines give you an indication of the future price trend.

- A three-point channel suggests where price could go.

42. Andrews Pitchfork

I prefer a technique called Andrews pitchfork to draw a channel. Begin with three consecutive turning points of similar magnitude. For the most recent two, draw a line connecting them. I show that in Figure 5.15 as the swing from H to G, although the line may be difficult to see.

Draw another line from the start of the price trend, F in this case, to an imaginary point midway between G and H (the middle is really the average of prices at G and H) and extend it into the future, I. The FI line is called the median line, and it represents the handle of the pitchfork. Complete the pitchfork by drawing the outer tines parallel to the median line, at G and H (forming tines GK and HJ).

In a rising price trend, two of the swing points should be minor lows. In a falling price trend, two of the turning points should be minor highs. Some use touches of the higher and lower Bollinger bands to pick two of the swing points with the third one coming from the start of the price trend.

The idea behind Andrews pitchfork is that price will tend to remain between the outer tines of the pitchfork. Thus, the lines mark support and resistance areas. If price pierces the lower channel line, GK, in a rising price trend, it means price has burrowed through support. If price pierces line HJ in a falling price trend, it means price has broken through overhead resistance. Penetration of either line as described means a change in the short- to intermediate-term price trend.

If price ventures outside the pitchfork, reenters and crosses the median line, then consider closing out the trade.

Market tops frequently occur at or between the top two lines, and market bottoms appear at or between the bottom two lines. Short-term reversals occur when price touches or nears the median line. A reversal at the centerline can be a good place to enter or add to existing positions.

The inset in Figure 5.15 shows two trading techniques using Andrews pitchfork. In the left figure, price moves from the top tine forming a pivot (turning point) at L and approaches but does not touch the median line at M. A strong up move follows.

The reverse of that appears for upward price trends. Price pivots at N but does not touch the median line O before reversing. The following move tends to be strong.

Ron Jaenisch (October 1996) describes the rule: "When prices form a pivot but do not reach the median line, they often make up for it when they form the next pivot by traveling even further in the opposite direction."

- Price tends to remain between the outer tines of the pitchfork, showing support or resistance.
- When price pierces one of the outer tines, it means a change in the short- to intermediate-term trend.
- If price climbs above the top tine and then reenters the pitchfork, crossing below the median line, then consider selling.
- If price drops below the lower tine and then reenters the pitchfork, crossing above the median line, then close out a short position.
- Tops in a rising price trend tend to appear at or between the top two tines. Bottoms in a falling price trend appear at or between the bottom two tines.

- When a reversal occurs at the median line, consider entering a trade or adding to an existing one.
- When price attempts to touch the median line but fails at another turning point, look for a strong move in the opposite direction.

43. Beware Throwbacks and Pullbacks

A throwback occurs after an upward breakout from a chart pattern when price rises and then returns to or near the breakout price or trendline boundary within a month. Separation between the chart pattern and price often leaves a small amount of white space as price rounds over. A pullback is the same idea, but after a downward breakout with price pulling back to the breakout or trendline boundary.

Throwbacks and pullbacks are important chart patterns. Novice traders unaware of their existence may close out positions at inopportune times, taking a loss just before price resumes the breakout direction.

Figure 5.16 shows an example of a throwback. Price breaks out of a symmetrical triangle when it closes above the top trendline and peaks

FIGURE 5.16 A throwback from a symmetrical triangle represents a pause in the upward move.

at A before curling around and heading back to the chart pattern in the throwback. When price nears the level of the triangle's apex at B, it finds support and resumes the upward move.

The AB move is the throwback. Although throwbacks take many shapes, the typical configuration appears in the inset. I used 26,542 chart patterns covering over two decades and found that 55 percent of those with upward breakouts had throwbacks.

After breaking out of a chart pattern, price climbs for an average of six days, rising 8 percent above the breakout price (measured from the breakout price to the highest high before price throws back). Then price curls over, leaving white space (C) on the chart and taking 10 days to return to the breakout price or trendline boundary. After that, 65 percent of the time price continues higher. By definition, a throwback must complete within a month.

Keep in mind that the numbers are averages. The Intersil throwback shown in Figure 5.16 peaked in two days and returned to the breakout price the next day, although it took two additional days for it to bottom at B.

- Throwbacks occur about half the time in chart patterns, returning the stock back to the breakout price within a month.

Figure 5.17 shows an example of a pullback. Price breaks out downward and eases lower to A before pulling back to the triangle apex. Eventually, price peaks at B before making a straight-line run downward.

The inset shows the average configuration of a pullback based on the same study of chart patterns. Pullbacks occur 57 percent of the time and take an average of six days to drop 9 percent. Then price begins a recovery, taking a total of 11 days to return to the breakout price. After that, just 47 percent of them continue lower. A pullback must finish within a month.

- A pullback occurs just over half the time, returning the stock back to the trendline boundary or breakout price before it resumes its downward move.

As Figures 5.16 and 5.17 show, price makes a move in the breakout direction, but then reverses before working its way back to the original breakout direction. This type of fake out catches novice traders by surprise, whipping them out of their investment for a loss. Do not be fooled. Expect the unexpected.

The experienced swing trader catches the breakout and rides it for a few days, cashing out before the reversal begins. When the throwback or

FIGURE 5.17 This pullback sees a recovery that overshoots the top of the pattern before resuming the downward price trend.

pullback completes, they jump in again and hold the stock for a resumption of the breakout move.

44. Triangle Apex Predicts Turns

I first learned about price turning at the apex of a triangle from Frost and Prechter (Wiley, 1999). **Figure 5.18** shows an example of an ascending triangle formed by a horizontal top trendline and an up-sloping trendline along the valleys. The two trendlines join at the apex, C.

I drew a vertical line down from the peak at A to B just to show how close the apex is to the peak.

Is it a coincidence that the two align almost perfectly? That is what I wanted to know, so I decided to test it.

Visual Test   I performed three tests. The first used 388 stocks and found 221 ascending, descending, and symmetrical triangles from October 30, 2006, to January 27, 2008. I drew the triangle trendline boundaries carefully

Johnson and Johnson (Medical Supplies, JNJ)

FIGURE 5.18 Price peaks near the apex of an ascending triangle.

and counted how often the apex was within a few days of a minor high or low. In 75 percent of the cases, the apex was near the turning point.

- Price formed a peak or valley within a few days of a triangle apex 75 percent of the time.

Automated Test   In the second test, I let my computer automatically draw the trendlines, meaning it was not as accurate as the first test. In this test, I was not looking for matches between the triangle apex and minor highs or lows, but major turns in the price trend. I visually compared the price trend before the triangle apex and after it. A direction change occurred 60 percent of the time.

For example, Figure 5.18 would show success in the first test when price nearly matched the apex at A and C. In the second test, it would also show success since price climbed up to A and then moved lower to sideways after C.

- Price changed direction 60 percent of the time within a few days of the triangle apex.

Math Test The last test used a different database spanning from July 1991 to July 1996 of known good chart patterns in 500 stocks. I found the nearest peak or valley within a month of each triangle's apex. The average distance from a peak or valley to the apex was 3.6 days. This compares to the average distance between *all* peaks or valleys of 13.1 days. Half that, or 6.55 days, would be the average distance if standing midway between the peak or valley. In other words, the 3.6-day average is closer than chance (6.55 days) suggests.

* The average distance from peak or valley to the triangle apex is 3.6 days.

45. Volume Preceding the Breakout

In many chart patterns, volume trends downward from the start of the pattern to the end like a wedge placed under a door to keep it open.

Volume tends to diminish even more a few days before the breakout. **Figure 5.19** shows an example. As the symmetrical triangle forms, notice that volume trends downward (C). A few days before the breakout, it drops

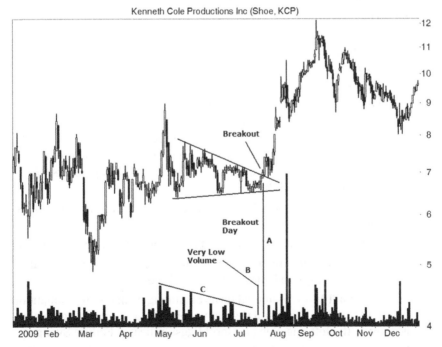

FIGURE 5.19 Volume trends downward and becomes very low a few days before the breakout.

even more, and that is an indication that the breakout is coming (line B). Then the breakout occurs at A. I drew vertical line A between price and volume, showing how they line up. In this case, volume hardly budged as price closed outside the top trendline, and that is unusual.

- Volume tends to hit very low levels a few days before the breakout.

CHAPTER CHECKLIST

This chapter shared many tips on stock market behavior that you can use to improve your trading or investing. Below is a checklist that may help.

☐ If price stalls near an old high or low, it could reverse. See (1) Timing the Exit: The 2B Rule.

☐ Busted patterns slightly underperform regular chart patterns. See (2) Busted Patterns for Profit.

☐ Stock performance improves if the busted direction aligns with the price trend shown by the industry and general market. See (2) Busted Patterns for Profit.

☐ Fibonacci extensions are no more accurate than any other tool for determining where price might reverse. See (4) Myth: Fibonacci Extensions Work!

☐ Divergence hints of a coming price turn. Look for divergence along the peaks in a rising price trend and along the valleys in a falling trend. See (5) Is Indicator Divergence a Dud?

☐ On the RSI indicator, look for divergence when it signals an overbought or oversold condition (locations where a price reversal is more likely) with two turning points about a month to six weeks apart. See (5) Is Indicator Divergence a Dud?

☐ Bullish divergence fails to beat the market more often than it works. See Testing Divergence.

☐ Only bullish divergence works and only in a bull market. See Table 5.1.

☐ If the RSI indicator remains shallow during divergence, performance improves, but only in a bear market. See Table 5.2.

☐ Look for small M- or W-shaped turns beginning from the overbought or oversold regions. It is best if the right peak is below—or the right valley is above—the left one. See (7) Good Eggs: Indicator Failure Swings.

☐ Use the linear scale to look for flat bases on the weekly or monthly charts. See (8) Flat Base Entry Pattern.

☐ Area gaps appear in congestion regions on high volume, but price fills the gap quickly and continues consolidating. See Area Gaps.

☐ Breakaway gaps appear as price leaves a consolidation region on high volume. The gap does not close quickly. See Breakaway Gaps.

☐ Continuation gaps appear near the middle of a straight-line run, often on high volume. See Continuation Gaps.

☐ Exhaustion gaps appear at the end of trends, on high volume, and close quickly. See Exhaustion Gaps.

☐ See How to Trade Gaps for a list of trading tips.

☐ A violent reversal sometimes occurs after an exhaustion gap. See How to Trade Gaps.

☐ If the market hands you a gain, take it to the bank. See (10) The Never Lose Pattern: The Inverted Dead-Cat Bounce.

☐ If the S&P or Nasdaq futures make a big move, either higher or lower, expect the stock market to open accordingly. See (11) What Are the Futures Doing?

☐ After price jumps higher, if it closes at the high for the day, place a limit order to sell the next day at 1.38 percent above the close. See Table 5.3.

☐ Bullish tails appear at minor lows as price spikes below the adjacent price bars, but close near the high. They signal a move higher. See Table 5.4.

☐ Bearish tails appear at minor highs like a lone tree on a hill. They mean a downturn is coming. They are not as reliable as bullish tails. See Table 5.4.

☐ Price fails to make a lower low or higher high the day after a tall (twice the one-month average height) price bar at least 68 percent of the time. See Table 5.5.

☐ After a tall price bar, price shows a slight tendency to close lower the next day. See Table 5.5.

☐ Use ugly double bottoms to detect a change from bear to bull. See (15) Ugly Double Bottom: A Higher Bottom.

☐ When many stocks show pipe bottoms, look for a bounce leading to a second bottom. That second bottom may spell the end of the bear market. See (16) Bullish Chart Patterns Appear.

☐ When brokers downgrade stocks across the board and upgrade few, the end of the bear market could be near. See Table 5.6.

☐ If the S&P 500 index is down 50 percent from the high, it is near bottom. See (18) You Feel Like Selling Everything.

☐ Volume spikes at bear market bottoms. See (19) High Volume Bottom.

☐ When good news lifts the market and bad news has little effect, expect the end of a bear market. See (20) Bad News Moves Nothing, Good News Lifts Market.

☐ A partial rise predicts a downward breakout. A partial decline predicts an upward breakout. See (21) Getting in Early: Partial Rises and Declines.

☐ After an upward breakout from a chart pattern, holding a stock for up to three pattern widths tends to see the best gains in the shortest time. See Table 5.7.

☐ After a downward breakout from a chart pattern, shorting the stock for longer than two pattern widths gives little extra return for the risk involved. See Table 5.7.

☐ Price drops faster than it rises. See (23) Price Drops Faster than It Rises.

☐ Think of what price will do in the future by reflecting price movement around a peak or valley. See (24) Mirrors for Trend Prediction.

☐ Reflect the vertical distance across a trendline to help predict how far price will drop. See (25) Trendline Mirrors: Another Reflection.

☐ Avoid investing in stocks showing a price mountain. See (26) Avoid Price Mountains.

☐ On average, it can take over five years for price to recover after a price mountain. See How Long to Summit a Price Mountain?

☐ When contemplating a trading decision, what would you tell your parents to do with a similar holding? See Fourteen Selling Tips You Need to Know.

☐ Use a stop loss order for short-term trades. See (27) Use Stops.

☐ At what price will the market tell me I am making a mistake? See (28) Sell When Wrong.

☐ If a stock makes an adverse or unexpected move, sell it. See (29) Sell on the Unexpected.

☐ If a stock drops 20 percent from a high, sell it. See (30) Sell on Trend Change.

☐ Sell a blue chip when it drops 10 percent from a peak. See (31) Sell Blue Chips 10 Percent Down.

☐ Understand your indicator tools so that when they say sell, you believe it. See (32) Indicator Says Sell: Obey It.

☐ Overlay your indicators on the same price chart to see if they signal at the same time. Remove duplicates. See (32) Indicator Says Sell: Obey It.

☐ If you followed your trading rules, would you make more money? See (33) Follow Your Rules.

☐ Sell if a bearish chart pattern confirms as valid. See (34) Sell on Confirmation of Bearish Pattern.

☐ Use the measure rule to gauge how far price is likely to move. See (35) Sell on Price Target.

☐ Convert the predicted rise or decline into a percentage to see if the move makes sense. See (35) Sell on Price Target.

☐ If price closes below support, then determine where price might stop declining. If support is nearby, then expect a pullback. See (36) Sell on Piercing Support.

☐ Watch the behavior of stocks in the same industry as a clue to weakness or strength. See (37) Sell on Industry Weakness.

☐ Look for deteriorating fundamentals, such as overhead increasing faster than sales or profits. See (38) Weak Fundamentals.

☐ Sell on hype. When everyone is talking about the latest gizmo, then the peak is near. Sell. See (39) Sell on Hype.

☐ When contemplating a sale, ask, *What would Tom do?* See (40) What Would Tom Do?

☐ A three-point channel suggests where price could go. See (41) Drawing Three-Point Channels.

☐ Use Andrews pitchfork to determine price trends. See (42) Andrews Pitchfork.

☐ Throwbacks occur about half the time in chart patterns, returning the stock back to the breakout price within a month. See (43) Beware Throwbacks and Pullbacks.

☐ A pullback occurs just over half the time, returning the stock back to the trendline boundary or breakout price before it resumes its downward move. See (43) Beware Throwbacks and Pullbacks.

☐ Price formed a peak or valley within a few days of a triangle apex 75 percent of the time. See Visual Test.

☐ Price changed direction 60 percent of the time within a few days of the triangle apex. See Automated Test.

☐ The average distance from peak or valley to the triangle apex is 3.6 days. See Math Test.

☐ Volume tends to hit very low levels a few days before the breakout. See (45) Volume Preceding the Breakout.

CHAPTER 6

Finding
and Fixing
What Is Wrong

When I worked for Tandy Corp, I handled the software development effort for an office telephone system. My boss and I sat down in a conference room and began discussing the project. About an hour later, he had to leave and told me to use the white board to map out the design.

I started drawing circles and labeling the states as *on hook, off hook*, and *conference*, with lines connecting them. After 15 minutes or so, I stopped to think about the design and discovered that once you boiled everything down, the phone was either on hook or off hook. Only those two states mattered. I knew my boss would not like the discovery, but I thought I had a strong case.

When he came back, it took all of 30 seconds for him to shoot it down. My two states had many others that it could be in, like *redialing, ringing, holding,* and so on. By the time we were done, we filled the eight-foot long white board with circles and lines.

I feel the same way when reviewing my trades at the end of each year. Traders can make four types of errors. They buy too early or too late, and they sell too early or too late. What else is there? Have I boiled down the problem too far such that when you answer the phone, it keeps ringing? That actually happened, but it was a hardware problem. To a software developer, *everything* is a hardware problem!

I developed a spreadsheet to help other traders analyze those four cases and put it on my website. Then I read an article by Peter Kaplan (September 2006). My four states became 13, and I am sitting here scratching my head, wondering how I missed them all.

I still like my four states, but in the interest of finding and fixing trading errors, what follows may help.

WHAT WAS THE MARKET BEHAVIOR?

After years of trading chart patterns, I realized how important the market trend is to the success of a trade. In *Fundamental Analysis and Position Trading*, Chapter 19 (see the section titled "What is Market Influence on Stocks?"), I will discuss research that says a stock follows the market higher or lower 64 percent of the time. Why would you go against those odds?

- Increase odds of success and profitability by trading with the trend.

It does not matter how much the market trended *before* entering the trade only to see it reverse after placing money on the table. Guessing correctly that the market has turned in a direction that supports a trade is important to success. I will discuss proof later.

For completed trades, assess how the market fared while holding the stock. Compare the closing price of the S&P 500 index on the day you sold to the day you bought. If the market is up a lot over those two points (or down a lot), then the market trended, suggesting it acted like a swift current pulling your boat along for the ride. If the market moved little then that suggests a sideways or trading range market. A trading range market is not bad for swing traders, but you still need to surf either an up or down wave.

What you are looking for is a way to determine the market's future direction before you buy.

- Did the trade direction (long in an up market, short in a down market) agree with the market direction?

One easy way to guess the future market trend is to determine the current trend and expect it to continue. Moving averages can help. For example, a nine period moving average will help smooth out the noise and show the underlying short-term trend. A rising market will show an upward-sloping moving average; a falling market will have a downward-sloping one.

- Use a moving average to help determine the market trend.

You can pick the moving average length and type for your trading style (I prefer a simple moving average). Day and swing traders may want to use a fast responding moving average like nine periods (periods means "price bars" for day traders and "days" for swing traders). Position traders may want to use a 50- or 200-day moving average, depending on their anticipated hold time.

Another way to determine the moving average length is to compute the average hold time for trades that last a year or less (for swing and position traders). For me, that is 86 calendar days. Divide by two (one cycle lasts two periods), and convert it to trading days.

There are approximately 21 trading days each month (252 days per year, but it varies from year to year). So I would test a 33-day moving average to see how it performed (86 ÷ 2 = 43 calendar days or about six weeks, which is 33 trading days). Using a 33-day moving average will help me decide the condition of the current market trend and help gauge whether the trend will continue (and for how long).

For buy-and-hold investors, since the market rises over the long term, it is helpful to determine the market trend, but during the life of the trade, the market will trend up or down for extended periods. Try to pick stocks near the end of a bear market (if you can tell when that is) or near the start of a bull one.

- Is overhead resistance nearby that might limit a move?

Look for overhead resistance in the market average (such as the S&P 500 index) to determine how long the trend might continue. Remember that price will eventually tunnel its way through overhead resistance.

Since the market is one force among many pushing price along, you may find that the industry to which the stock belongs exerts more pressure on the stock than the general market. That is what my testing found, and I explore that later.

WAS THE INDUSTRY TRENDING?

Assess the industry trend. I count the number of stocks moving higher versus those moving lower in the same industry before I buy a stock.

For example, when I considered buying stock in Coldwater Creek (CWTR), I found that 16 apparel retailing stocks were trending higher, and three were dropping. That told me the industry was bullish, and I expected the general market to move up, too.

Another way to determine industry direction is to find an exchange traded fund (ETF) or sector fund that covers the industry you are interested in buying. For example, if I wanted to buy Advanced Micro Devices (AMD), a maker of semiconductors, I might choose the semiconductor HOLDRs

(SMH) as representative of the industry. If that ETF is climbing, then it suggests a prospering industry.

- Compare the trend of stocks in the same industry or use an ETF/sector fund that represents the industry.

Compare the sector fund or ETF with the appropriate market index (Nasdaq for tech stocks, S&P for everything else). I divide the price of the ETF by the index for a relative strength test. If the tech stock is outperforming the index, which is what I am looking for, then a line chart will show the ratio moving higher. If the market is beating the ETF, then the line will slope downward. A one-month moving average of the ratio helps gauge the trend in choppy conditions.

- Compare your industry ETF or sector fund with the general market and buy industries that are rising faster than the market (showing better relative strength).

Does a Rising Tide Really Lift All Boats?

To determine whether a rising market and industry really helps, I decided to test it. The results appear in **Table 6.1**.

I used all of my completed trades, but excluded:

- Those for which I no longer had price data
- Day trades
- Short sales
- Non-stock trades (like trades in options or ETFs)
- Long-term investments (gains between 1,000 and 5,000 percent skewed the results)
- Trades in which the industry trend could not be determined (such as when three stocks trended higher and three lower)

That left 357 trades.

When the general market, as represented by the S&P 500 index, posted a higher close during the trade and the majority of other stocks in the same

TABLE 6.1 Average Gain or Loss by Market and Industry Direction

Market	S&P Up	S&P Down
Industry Up	15%	7%
Industry Down	−7%	−10%

industry also posted higher closes, I made an average of 15 percent. When both the market and industry dropped during the trade, I lost 10 percent. If the industry was down, but the market climbed, I still lost 7 percent. Finally, if the trends reversed—the market fell, but the industry climbed—I made 7 percent.

There is my proof of industry and market influence. The best performance comes when both the industry and market are moving higher during a trade. In second place is when the industry is moving up, but the market is not. In other words, the industry trend is more important than the market trend, at least for my trades.

Substituting the median performance for the average (to remove the risk of large gains or losses influencing the results) does not change the trend. The industry trend remains more important than the markets, and having both the market and industry trending higher helped results. A rising tide lifts all boats, and a receding tide lowers all boats.

If I include nearly all trades, especially those held longer than a year, the percentages change, but not the trend.

- Improve profitability by trading with the market and industry trends.
- The industry trend is more important than the market trend.

Knowing the industry and market trends before trading (and hoping the trends continue throughout the trade) is important, but they might not help if you botch the entry.

HOW IS THE TIMING?

For each trade, ask yourself if you entered too early, too late, or hit it spot on. That is often easy to assess when trading chart patterns since the breakout is where price changes from moving sideways to trending. The breakout is the perfect entry price.

However, other types of entries will work as well. Throwbacks or pullbacks, for example, offer another chance to enter the trade at a good price. I also mentioned a shelf—a flat area on the right bottom of a double bottom—as another entry possibility. In fact, many acceptable entry positions can occur during each trade, providing your trading plan allows for them.

Early Entry

Let us review early entry first. Do you consistently enter trades too early, meaning you *think* the stock is going to breakout upward so you buy before that happens? On those trades, did you make more money, or did the failure rate increase?

In other words, you can evaluate your results two ways: higher profit or increased risk. If a stock is going to reach 10, then the sooner (lower price) you buy in, the better. If you buy in sooner, then a stop loss order might be closer to the optimum buy price, but that could increase the risk of failure (if the stock trips the stop because the stop is so close). Of course, if the stock does not hit 10 then you could be in trouble. If you buy before confirmation (before the breakout from a chart pattern) and the pattern fails to confirm, then the trade could post a loss.

- Did you enter the trade too early, too late, or just right?

Entering a trade using chart patterns is easy, since the breakout price is often known in advance. It may be difficult to place a buy order on a sloping trendline, for example, so I allow one day to close above the trendline, confirming the chart pattern and staging a breakout, and buy at the open the next day. That is what I call a perfect entry.

Late Entry

I did research on my trades and found that when I entered a trade more than 5 percent above where I was supposed to enter, I made less money and increased the risk of failure. I found that if I chased a stock higher, such as one breaking out and moving in a straight-line run up, I often bought just before price reversed.

Do you have the same problem? Do not count waiting for a throwback as a late entry unless you blow that, too. Some traders only enter after a throwback completes. That way, they are not caught owning a stock that returns to the breakout price and then continues its skydiver impersonation.

- Do not chase a stock. If you cannot buy within 5 percent of the breakout (optimum entry price), then skip the trade or wait for a retrace.

Early and Late Exits

Exits are more difficult to gauge. When I examined my completed trades, it became obvious where price peaked on the chart. If I exited before that peak, then I sold too soon. That meant I cut my potential profit short. However, selling *after* the peak was worse. It is like opening your wallet or purse and dumping out any change you find, and then shoveling out the bills as well. It is money you have, in hand, that you are throwing away.

Figure 6.1 shows an example of a utility stock I owned, split into two pieces so it would fit on one figure. After waiting for the 2007 to 2009 bear market to end, I finally bought the stock eight days after it bottomed. Point A shows the approximate price and date, and B shows the bear market low.

It took time to recognize that the general market and stock had bottomed. Although the chart shows that I bought late, I consider this a perfect entry since picking it so close to the end of a bear market is a wonderful gift of timing.

The exit is another matter. Price peaked at D, and that would have been the perfect exit. Since this was a long-term holding, I was not in any rush to sell. However, the stock during 2010 had not moved much, and when price plunged below the 30-week moving average and out of stage three (see Chapter 16 in *Fundamental Analysis and Position Trading*, the section titled, "The Weinstein Setup," for an explanation), I decided to sell. Point C shows the location. I consider this a late exit. I missed selling at the peak by one month and four dollars per share. Ouch.

In a similar manner, I evaluated all of my trades between January 2000 and September 2010. **Table 6.2** shows the results, but it excludes day

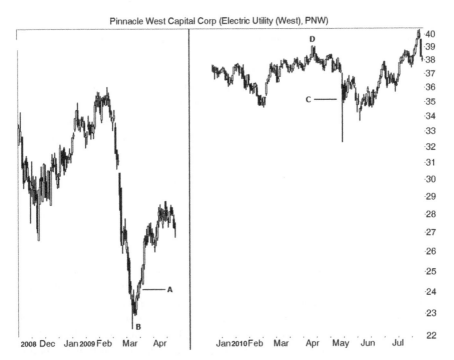

FIGURE 6.1 Entry and exit timing for this utility stock.

TABLE 6.2   Trade Analysis for Entry and Exit Timing

	Early Entry	Perfect Entry	Late Entry	Early Exit	Perfect Exit	Late Exit
Distribution	17%	63%	20%	34%	30%	35%
Gain/Loss	2%	5%	−3%	7%	6%	−5%

trades, short sales, options, and ETF trades. In other words, it shows only recent stock trades.

The distribution row shows a frequency distribution for entries and another for exits, expressed as a percentage. For example, 17 percent of the entries were too early, resulting in average gains of 2 percent. When I bought later than I should have, which happened 20 percent of the time, I lost 3 percent. Perfectly timed trades resulted in gains of 5 percent. That may sound low, but the numbers include two bear markets and exclude my biggest gains so as not to skew the results.

The numbers show that I am good at timing the buy. That is easy when a chart pattern is involved (buy at the breakout), but the trades also include other situations, such as buying more of a stock, buying when it breaks out of a consolidation region, or after a throwback completes.

On the exit side, 34 percent of the time I exited the trade too soon, but gained an average of 7 percent. When I held too long, which occurred 35 percent of the time, I lost 5 percent.

For my trading style, it is better to enter and exit a trade early than late. Notice how the numbers are about a third of the time for each exit condition. The numbers suggest that I have a good system for entry, but not for exiting. Of the two, exiting is more important, and that is where I am weakest.

Study an analysis of your own trades to find clues to how you can improve your timing.

- Holding a trade too long is worse than selling too early.

ARE ALL ENTRY CONDITIONS MET?

If you use a system for trading, are you following the rules? Do you jump the gun and buy before your system signals an entry? Analyzing your trades can tell whether that is a good thing. Likely, it is bad for profitability.

In the review of my chart pattern trades, it is seldom that I do not wait for a breakout. However, when I try to bottom fish, I am often early. In other words, I *think* the stock has bottomed, so I buy only to find that I was too early by weeks or months. That can be a costly mistake. As Table 6.2 shows, I earn less by entering a trade early than if the timing is right.

Let me share a story with you. A person I will call Fred sent me a chart of XYZ (a fictitious symbol). "I am a student who has saved up a bit of money to invest and cannot pass this great opportunity by," he wrote.

Judging by that sentence alone, do you get the feeling that he is going to get slaughtered? He is in love with the stock already and does not even own it. What happens when price goes against his belief? He is going to maintain his bullish stance because (he writes), "I know XYZ is a good buy." He will finally throw in the towel just as the stock bottoms, costing him dearly not only in money but pride as well.

But there is something I have not told you about him. He has to wait a week or two to transfer the cash into his account. Maybe the stock will climb out of sight by then or tumble, proving his *great opportunity* as nothing more than novice overconfidence.

What does this anecdote have to do with entry conditions? Do not trade unless properly capitalized. If you have not got the bucks, then paper trade it. That is what I told Fred to do.

- Never fall in love with a stock.
- Is each trade properly capitalized?

Overconfidence: My Worst Trades

My worst trades are those in which I *know* I am right. Usually the feeling happens when I have had six or more consecutively winning trades. "Trading is an easy game. Everything I buy turns to gold!" That is when I throw caution to the wind and make an outsized bet on a stock that cannot lose. "I know it's going up;" only it drops faster than a hot air balloon out of propane. I hold on, knowing the stock will soon turn around and then double, fulfilling my prediction. Only it does not.

Two weeks before the stock bottoms, I sell, taking a massive hit. It is surprising how often it plays out that way.

I struggled with this behavior pattern early in my trading career until I figured out what was wrong. Now, I grow cautious and either skip questionable trades or cut the position size.

Another technique I use is to avoid looking at how much money I am making. That way, I do not gloat about the string of winners. I consider each trade as another opportunity for the market to prove me wrong, so I proceed cautiously.

If you use indicators to qualify a purchase, then wait for the signals to occur before buying. *Knowing* that an indicator will signal within a day or two is different than actually seeing it trigger. Buying a stock before all of the entry conditions are met is a good way to lose money.

- Be careful trading after a string of winners. The overconfidence could produce a big loss.
- Wait for all entry conditions to trigger before buying.

WAS THE POSITION SIZE PROPER?

I have already discussed position sizing in Chapter 2, Money Management, but if you are leveraging your trades and taking hits like a silhouette on the shooting range, then it is time to reevaluate. As I mentioned, in a bear market, I cut my position size to as much as one-eighth of what it was during a bull market. When the bear market ended, I ramped up the trade size, but that took time.

I like having many securities in my portfolio because of the diversity. That means a smaller position size per holding than what I used to trade. I also use volatility-based position sizing (see Table 2.2 and discussion).

If you have rules for position sizing and follow them, then this should not be an issue. You may double up on a position now and again, but check on how well the trade worked. If you increased the position size and panicked, then that is bad.

In *Fundamental Analysis and Position Trading*, Chapter 21 (the section titled "The Intel Fiasco"), I share with you how I panicked when trading Intel. I cut the position size in half before the market opened, but it still drew blood. If you are interested in buying the movie rights, then we can work something out.

- Did you size each position properly?

WAS AN INITIAL STOP USED?

If I invest (buy-and-hold, but many position trades as well), then I do not use a stop unless I want to sell the position. In that case, I will often use a trailing stop placed a penny below the prior day's low. In a strong uptrend, the stop will ride price higher, but I know that as soon as momentum weakens, I will be cashed out.

For day trades, the time required to confirm the placement of a stop loss order can be an issue. Instead of placing a hard stop, I will use a mental one. If a stock turns in an adverse direction, I will sell it immediately instead of letting a hard stop take me out. Using a mental stop allows me to focus on the trade instead of worrying if the stop order went through and then trailing it upward.

For swing trades, though, it is entirely different. I use a stop on every trade. I am in the trade for the short term with diminished profit potential, so I want to keep losses manageable.

The start of a trade is the most dangerous time. The initial stop can be far from the entry price, especially for highly volatile stocks. If the trade goes bad, it will cause a big loss, and those losses are the worst. You have just entered a trade with the hope and confidence that it is going to be a huge winner only to find hopes dashed when the pinheads push the stock down just enough to tag the stop.

When checking trades for mistakes, was the initial stop positioned properly? Did you ignore the stop? Read Chapter 3 of this volume, Do Stops Work?, if you have difficulty answering the first question.

- Was an initial stop used?
- Was the stop positioned properly?
- Did you ignore the stop or remove it?

DID YOU EXIT BEFORE THE STOP?

In *rare* situations (maybe three times per 500 trades), I will lower the stop (often due to questionable placement) or remove it altogether.

For long-term trades, sometimes I will use a stop for a while when I think the stock is going to reverse, and I have doubled my money. I want to capture the double, so I put a stop in place. When the stock resumes its upward push, giving profits a comfortable cushion, I will remove the stop.

After placing the initial stop and assuming the stock moves up, did you raise the stop? Keeping a stop properly positioned as the stock climbs is a wonderful way to *cut your losses and let your profits ride*. I am sure you have heard that phrase.

When I started using stops on every trade, I was surprised. I knew it would cut my losses, but I was also pleased to discover that I gave back less profit. It is aggravating to see a large gain dwindle and then disappear altogether when a rising stock reverses and turns into a loss. You look back at the chart and ask, "How could that happen? Why didn't I sell at the top?" Using a trailing stop helps prevent the profit giveback.

- Did you use a trailing stop?
- Was the stop properly positioned?
- Did you exit before the stop triggered?

Have you ever looked at a chart and said, "This trade is going to be stopped out"? Price is trending down, other stocks in the industry are melting like ice cubes in a frying pan, and the market is in freefall. The inner voice that develops with experience says, "Sell now!"

In the dozen or so times when that has happened, I have changed the stop into a market order. It worked, saving me money. However, preempting a stop should not become a habit! Do not sell a stock just because it is near a stop. Many stocks I have owned have bottomed a penny or two above the stop and then gone on to be winners. Allow the stock every opportunity to move higher, but if it is clear that it is going to hit the stop, then sell the dog.

- Sometimes selling early is smart; just do not let it become a habit.

WHAT WAS THE RISK/REWARD RATIO?

I am not a big fan of the risk/reward ratio, but it seems to be a hit among traders and educators. When I place a stop, I know in advance what my risk is: It is the difference between what I will pay when I buy the stock and the stop (assuming it does not gap lower). What about the reward? There is the rub.

How high will the stock go? Will it soar by three or four times the risk, as many claim a winning trade should? How many times have you thrown away a stock that went on to double because it had less than a 4 to 1 risk/reward ratio (the reward is the first number, by convention)?

That is why I do not care for the risk/reward ratio. I can accurately gauge the loss, but not the reward. However, when setting up a short-term trade like a swing trade where I will pick a price target to sell at, then the ratio is important. I want to maximize my gains for the capital employed. Knowing how much I will make in a swing trade is important information. But for longer trades, I let my profits run and do not concern myself with the risk/reward ratio.

If you are contemplating a trade with defined profit and loss targets and the risk to reward ratio is less than three or four to one, then consider looking elsewhere for another opportunity. The reward is just not high enough to justify the risk of loss. To put it a different way, the reward has to be high enough to compensate for losing trades.

Another trade will come along that will have the right setup conditions. That will be the trade to take. The pros wait for the right conditions before trading. You should, too.

- Ignore the risk to reward ratio when you cannot accurately determine the reward.
- For trades with profit targets, use a risk to reward ratio of three or four (or higher) to one.
- The reward must be high enough to compensate for losing trades.

DID YOU AVERAGE UP?

We discovered in Chapter 2 that scaling in works, but only if the stock rises. That is how I trade some winning positions. I will buy more as the stock rises (averaging up) to bring a partial position size up to a full position.

For example, I bought more shares of CH Energy Group (CHG—it is in the process of being merged) at 39.72 since the yield was 5.4 percent and it was within a dollar of the yearly low. I sold when it hit 54, the top end of the trading range.

Another buy situation occurs when I have a position in a stock and as price rises, it forms a new chart pattern. If it breaks out downward, I will sell. If the breakout is upward, then I may add to an existing position. Admittedly, I am increasing risk and decreasing profit since I am buying at a higher price, but sometimes it is better than having the cash sitting around earning almost nothing.

Your trading plan should specify if and when to add to a position. Outline the conditions that will be necessary for another buy. If you add to a position when the trading plan either does not address the issue or says not to buy more, then that is a trading error.

- Does your trading plan allow for averaging up?
- When you averaged up, was it a profitable move?

DID YOU AVERAGE DOWN?

If you are a day or swing trader, then do not average down. I have already explained why in Chapter 2. For position traders and buy-and-hold investors, then buying when price drops to lower the average cost works, but only if the stock recovers.

My biggest loss—ever—came from a long-term investment in Gencorp (GY) when I bought the stock in 2007 before the bear market began and averaged down only once. In 2008, fearing the stock was heading toward bankruptcy, I finished selling my shares just three days before the stock bottomed. Three days! The stock moved sideways for eight months and then started recovering, quadrupling in price in five months.

I have averaged down just 6 percent of the time over 30 years and 55 percent of them were profitable, returning only $21 in average profits per trade. That return barely covers commissions, and it certainly does not justify the risk involved.

If your trading plan says an investment is worth buying more as price drops, then do so carefully. Watch your position size. For example, if you buy a position in a stock for $20,000 and it is worth $5,000 now, you may be tempted to throw another $15,000 to bring it back up to $20,000. That would mean an initial investment of $35,000 ($20,000 + $15,000), concentrating too much of your assets in one stock, even though current values say otherwise.

Should you decide to average down, then do so only once, and do not throw too much money into the stock. If you are right, the stock will recover, giving you a handsome return. If you are wrong, it will not hurt so much if the position remains small or sized properly with others in the portfolio.

- Only investors and position traders should average down, and only in rare situations.
- If you average down, then do so only *once* and add no more than 50 percent of your initial investment.

ARE YOU BUYING OUT OF SEASON?

This last item concerns timing. I traded an exchange traded fund in agriculture (called Powershares DB Agriculture, symbol: DBA) because I noticed that it often peaked in June. On June 1, the stock reached its high, just as I anticipated. What I did not know is that the fund would complicate my tax returns by sending me Schedule K-1 (partnership) because it trades futures contracts or straddles. Yuck.

I did an analysis of my trades by sorting them by purchase and sale dates and the median gain or loss (because large numbers skew an average). When I bought a stock in March, I made over 25 percent more money than buying in any other month (second place was September). If I sold in May, I more than doubled the second best month (January).

The best block of months to buy is harder to determine because no one block stands out. Clearly, buying in March or April outperforms the other months, but August and September also do well. The best block of months to sell was between January and May—preferably in May. That period resulted in the highest gains while the other months showed losses.

Based on my trades, I should avoid buying from October to February (but December is a good month), and May through July. I will want to avoid selling from June to December.

Perhaps you have heard the phrase, *Sell in May and go away*. The analysis of my trades supports that belief since May is the most profitable time to sell. March and September are the best times to buy.

Analyze your trades to see what trends you can uncover. If you have difficulty making money trading in June, then perhaps that is the time to schedule a vacation. September is historically the worst performing month of the year, so that might be the time to back up the 18-wheeler and fill it with new stocks.

- Sell in May and go away.
- Based on your trades, are certain months better for trading than others?

TRADING CHECKLIST

When I was growing up, I wrote a diary into which I poured my feelings, captured my thoughts, and explored my dreams. I destroyed it. As an investor, position or swing trader, I plan every trade and write down my thoughts before each trade begins. As a day trader, I still plan the trading day, but often do not have time to journal each trade. I add my thoughts after the trading day ends or between trades.

Why bother? There is an old joke that goes, "Experience allows you to recognize a mistake when you make it again." Having a trading journal allows you to build upon success or spot bad habits before they become a serious problem.

Here is the checklist I follow when contemplating buying a security. This is the trader's equivalent of a pilot's checklist and is just as important. Some of what is described here will be explained later in the other books in this series. If it is unclear now, do not worry about it.

- ☐ Today's date: This is the date I plan the trade, not the date a buy occurs. I may actually buy the stock weeks later—or not at all.
- ☐ Suggested maximum position size: My computer determines the position size according to how far down from the yearly high the price has dropped. The larger the decline, the smaller the position size in a nod that the market might be turning bearish.
- ☐ Order details: This includes the number of shares, order type, and buy price.
- ☐ Date bought: If the trade executes, the details are here.

☐ Stop: 25.58 – 4.6 percent. Stop used: The numbers shown are from a sample stock. My program automatically computes a volatility stop for me. The *stop used* phrase is for the actual stop price used, which can differ from a volatility-based stop.

☐ SAR and upside target: This identifies underlying support and overhead resistance areas (SAR), and how much I want to make from the trade (upside target).

☐ Score: For a chart pattern trade, this uses the scoring system to evaluate how well the chart pattern might perform. This is covered in *Fundamental Analysis and Position Trading*.

☐ Weinstein stage: This is a number from 1 to 4 that describes which stage the stock is in. Buying in stage 1 or 2 is better than in 3 or 4. See *Fundamental Analysis and Position Trading*, Chapter 16, the section titled "The Weinstein Setup".

☐ Next earnings: This serves as an important reminder to check the date of the next quarterly earnings announcement. I will not buy a stock closer than three weeks away unless I anticipate a short-duration trade.

☐ Weekly scale: I look at other time scales to help identify price trends and support and resistance zones.

☐ Indicators: I look at the Wilder relative strength index (RSI) and commodity channel index (CCI) to check for divergence and recent trading signals.

☐ My computer analyzes where in the yearly high-low range the stock is trading, and it makes a prediction of whether the stock will close higher or lower the next day. To do this, it measures the percentage change of the prior day and looks for similar moves in the past. When it finds one, it sees if the next day closed higher or lower. Then it tabulates all of those moves and reports its findings.

The program calculates the noise (trendiness) and how the stock, industry, and S&P have moved over the past one, three, and six months.

Finally, it tells whether the average volume is rising or falling over the past three weeks, compares the strength of the stock relative to the S&P 500 index, and suggests the best day to buy the stock based on up closes over the past two years.

☐ Trade type: day, swing, position, or buy and hold.

☐ Chart pattern traded: If I am trading a chart pattern, I identify it here.

☐ Buy reason: This is the big one. Why am I buying the stock? I discuss the buying strategy I am going to use, and how I see the trade playing out.

The sale checklist is shorter, consisting of the date of sale and the reason for it. The program also suggests the best day to sell, based on up closes.

Some traders construct their journals on a spreadsheet so they can statistically analyze their trades (win/loss ratio, cumulative profits, average winning and losing trades, and so on). I do that, too, by listing every trade.

- Use a buy and sell checklist so that important items are not forgotten.

CHAPTER CHECKLIST

This chapter discussed tips for finding what is wrong with trades and suggested solutions. *Proving* that a rising tide lifts all boats (stocks) was an interesting finding (Table 6.1), but knowing that the industry trend is more important than the market trend to making money is valuable information. That alone is worth the cost of this book.

In the next book of the series (*Fundamental Analysis and Position Trading*), we begin looking at value investing—having fun with fundamentals. Here is a checklist to review what we have discussed in this chapter.

☐ Increase odds of success and profitability by trading with the trend. See What Was the Market Behavior?

☐ Did the trade direction (long in an up market, short in a down market) agree with the market direction? See What Was The Market Behavior?

☐ Use a moving average to help determine the market trend. See What Was The Market Behavior?

☐ Is overhead resistance nearby that might limit a move? See What Was The Market Behavior?

☐ Compare the trend of stocks in the same industry or use an ETF/sector fund that represents the industry. See Was the Industry Trending?

☐ Compare your industry ETF or sector fund with the general market and buy industries that are rising faster than the market (showing better relative strength). See Was the Industry Trending?

☐ Improve profitability by trading with the market and industry trends. See Does a Rising Tide Really Lift All Boats?

☐ The industry trend is more important than the market trend. See Table 6.1.

☐ Did you enter the trade too early, too late, or just right? See Early Entry.

☐ Do not chase a stock. If you cannot buy within 5 percent of the breakout (optimum entry price), then skip the trade or wait for a retrace. See Late Entry.

☐ Holding a trade too long is worse than selling too early. See Table 6.2.

☐ Never fall in love with a stock. See Are All Entry Conditions Met?

☐ Is each trade properly capitalized? See Are All Entry Conditions Met?

☐ Be careful trading after a string of winners. The overconfidence could produce a big loss. See Overconfidence: My Worst Trades.

☐ Wait for all entry conditions to trigger before buying. See Overconfidence: My Worst Trades.

☐ Did you size each position properly? See Was the Position Size Proper?

☐ Was an initial stop used? See Was an Initial Stop Used?

☐ Was the stop positioned properly? See Was an Initial Stop Used?

☐ Did you ignore the stop or remove it? See Was an Initial Stop Used?

☐ Did you use a trailing stop? See Did You Exit Before the Stop?

☐ Was the trailing stop properly positioned? See Did You Exit Before the Stop?

☐ Did you exit before the stop triggered? See Did You Exit Before the Stop?

☐ Sometimes selling early is smart; just do not let it become a habit. See Did You Exit Before the Stop?

☐ Ignore the risk to reward ratio when you cannot accurately determine the reward. See What Was the Risk/Reward Ratio?

☐ For trades with profit targets, use a risk to reward ratio of 3 or 4 (or higher) to 1. See What Was the Risk/Reward Ratio?

☐ The reward must be high enough to compensate for losing trades.

☐ Does your trading plan allow for averaging up? See Did You Average Up?

☐ When you averaged up, was it a profitable move? See Did You Average Up?

☐ Only investors and position traders should average down, and only in rare situations. See Did You Average Down?

☐ If you average down, then do so only *once* and add no more than 50% of your initial investment. See Did You Average Down?

☐ Sell in May and go away. See Are You Buying Out of Season?

☐ Based on your trades, are certain months better for trading than others? See Are You Buying Out of Season?

☐ Use a trading checklist so that important items are not forgotten. See Trading Checklist.

CHAPTER 7

What We Learned

This chapter lists all of the discoveries I shared with you in these pages, sorted by chapter.

CHAPTER 1: HOW TO RETIRE AT 36

☐ Work hard and save every penny you earn at a job that pays a good salary.

☐ Live as cheaply as you can and invest your savings with care.

☐ Find stocks in which a buyout collapses. Buy when they bottom.

☐ Hold those stocks for the long term (I held some of Michaels Stores for 18 years).

CHAPTER 2: MONEY MANAGEMENT

☐ The introduction defines the terms, buy-and-hold, investor, position trader, swing trader, and day trader.

☐ How much do you need to trade or invest? Answer: $2,000 to $50,000. See the section Trading: How Much Money, Honey?

☐ For definitions on order types, see Order Types: Read the Fine Print!

☐ Read the fine print on how your broker handles the various types of orders. See Order Types: Read the Fine Print!

☐ Adjust the amount spent on each trade according to market conditions. See Table 2.1.

☐ After a bear market begins, cut the amount spent for new positions in half for each ten-percentage point decline in the S&P 500 index measured from the bull market peak. See Table 2.2.

☐ Size the amount to spend on each trade according to market conditions, adjust the amount spent for the stock's and market's volatility, and use a volatility stop to limit losses. See Position Sizing by Market Condition: Bull or Bear?

☐ The position sizing formula adjusts for market and stock volatility as well as market conditions (bull or bear). See Position Sizing by Market Condition: Bull or Bear?

☐ Hold as many positions as you can comfortably manage while maintaining diversity. See How Many Stocks to Hold?

☐ The number of positions in a portfolio can vary by trading style. See Table 2.3.

☐ Begin with a core portfolio of stocks and add stocks to trade depending on the trading style selected. See A Better Way? Portfolio Composition.

☐ How long should you hold a position to guarantee a profit? See Table 2.4.

☐ My best hold time is between three and four years long, but yours may vary. See Hold Time: My Trades.

☐ Determine when to buy, sell, or hold by the stock and market trends. See Table 2.5.

☐ Always trade with the trend. The general market, industry, and stock should all be trending the same way. See Stock Trending Down.

☐ Trading a constant position size can have disastrous results. See Table 2.6.

☐ Trading using fixed dollar amounts improves results, but not by much. See Table 2.7.

☐ A volatility based position size gives the best results . . . for rising stock prices. See Table 2.8.

☐ Using a trailing stop hurts profits but limits losses. See Testing Scaling In, Test 2.

☐ Raising a stop to breakeven is no guarantee of profitability. See Test 5.

☐ Scaling into a trade works only if the stock continues to rise. See Test 6.

☐ The success of averaging down depends on the hold time. See Tables 2.8 and 2.10.

☐ For scaling in and averaging down conclusions, see Scaling In and Averaging Down Summary.

☐ For tips on averaging down according to trading style, see Table 2.11.

☐ Table 2.12 shows the results when scaling out of trades.

☐ If price is rising, scaling out leaves money on the table. If price is dropping, scaling out means a larger loss than selling the entire position at once. See Scaling Out Summary.

☐ Invest a lump sum at once. Dollar cost averaging underperforms. See Dollar-Cost-Averaging: Good or Bad?

☐ Avoid using leverage unless you are a seasoned trader. See Using Leverage: An Expensive Lesson! and Leverage Guidelines Checklist.

☐ See Leverage Guidelines Checklist for a checklist when thinking of using leverage.

CHAPTER 3: DO STOPS WORK?

☐ What size gain is required to overcome a given loss? See Table 3.1.

☐ Hold time loss is the largest potential loss during a trade. See What Is Hold Time Loss?

☐ A mental stop is one kept in your head and not placed with a broker. Only seasoned traders should use mental stops. See Mental Stop: For Professionals Only!

☐ Avoid placing stops where other traders place theirs. See Minor High or Low Stop: A Good Choice.

☐ Avoid placing stops at round numbers (those ending in zero). See Squaring Off Round Numbers.

☐ Chart patterns represent good stop locations because they often act as future support and resistance areas. See Chart Pattern Stop: Too Costly?

☐ Measure the distance from the stop to the buy price to make sure it is not too far away. See Chart Pattern Stop: Too Costly?

☐ When price rises to a new high, place a stop directly below the prior minor low and below the moving average at that minor low. See Stopped by a Moving Average.

☐ Draw up-sloping trendlines along valleys, down-sloping trendlines along peaks. See The Truth About Trendlines.

☐ For other tips about trendlines, see The Truth About Trendlines.

☐ Use a trendline for stop placement. Trail a stop upward as price rises, beneath a trendline at the prior minor low. Tighten the stop if price moves sideways, forming a congestion region. See Trendline Stop.

☐ A Fibonacci stop is useful for straight-line runs where the prior minor low might be too far away from the current price. Set a stop below the 62 percent (or 67 percent, see below) retrace value. See Fibonacci Retrace Stop: Deal or Dud?

☐ Place a stop a penny or two below the 67 percent (not 62 percent) retrace of the prior move up. See Fibonacci Tests Contradiction.

☐ Fibonacci retracements offer no advantage over any other number as a turning point. See Fibonacci Tests Contradiction.

☐ A fixed percentage trailing stop uses a constant percentage below the *high water mark* as a stop price. See Fixed Percentage Trailing Stop.

☐ Learn how to calculate a volatility stop. See Volatility Stop.

☐ A volatility stop helps prevent a position from being stopped out on normal price fluctuations. See Volatility Stop.

☐ A chandelier stop hangs off the high price. See Chandelier Stop Leaves You Hanging.

☐ Table 3.4 shows the performance of various stop types.

☐ Stops cut profit more than they limit risk. See Results Summary.

☐ See Average True Range for details on calculating the true range.

☐ See Top Stop Exit for details on a trailing profit target stop.

☐ Use a volatility stop to determine how close to place a stop, how to hide the stop below a minor low where others cannot find it, and how tight consolidation regions make for good stop locations. See What I Use.

CHAPTER 4: SUPPORT AND RESISTANCE

☐ Resistance can become support that can become resistance. See Types of Support and Resistance.

☐ The first leg of a well-behaved measured move approximates the time and price move of the second leg. See Measured Move Support and Resistance.

☐ Price stops within the corrective phase of a measured move chart pattern 35 percent of the time in a bull market. See Table 4.1.

☐ Overhead resistance occurs at peaks 34 percent of the time. See Minor High Resistance.

☐ Peaks with volume half the average tend to show more overhead resistance than those with 1.5 times the average volume. See Volume at Minor High Resistance.

☐ Valleys show support 33 percent of the time. See Minor Low Support.

☐ Valleys with volume half the average tend to show more support than do those with volume 1.5 times the average. See Volume at Minor Low Support.

☐ Table 4.2 shows that support gets stronger over time.

☐ Table 4.3 shows that the strength of overhead resistance tends to remain constant over time.

☐ Gaps show support 20 percent of the time and resistance 25 percent of the time in a bull market. See Gaps Showing Support and Resistance.

☐ The middle of a tall candle is no more likely to show support or resistance than any other part. See Myth: Tall Candle Support and Resistance.

☐ See Horizontal Consolidation Regions for details about the stopping power of those regions.

☐ Price trends horizontally near a round number 22 percent of the time. See Another Look at Round Numbers.

☐ Price finds support in a straight-line run between 69 and 85 percent of the time. See Support in Straight-Line Runs.

☐ In a straight-line run downward, price sets up future resistance between 69 and 76 percent of the time. See Resistance in Straight-Line Runs.

☐ Table 4.4 shows a summary of support and resistance at technical features.

CHAPTER 5: 45 TIPS EVERY TRADER SHOULD KNOW

☐ If price stalls near an old high or low, it could reverse. See (1) Timing the Exit: The 2B Rule.

☐ Busted patterns slightly underperform regular chart patterns. See (2) Busted Patterns for Profit.

☐ Stock performance improves if the busted direction aligns with the price trend shown by the industry and general market. See (2) Busted Patterns for Profit.

☐ Fibonacci extensions are no more accurate than any other tool for determining where price might reverse. See (4) Myth: Fibonacci Extensions Work!

☐ Divergence hints of a coming price turn. Look for divergence along the peaks in a rising price trend and along the valleys in a falling trend. See (5) Is Indicator Divergence a Dud?

☐ On the RSI indicator, look for divergence when it signals an overbought or oversold condition (locations where a price reversal is more likely) with two turning points about a month to six weeks apart. See (5) Is Indicator Divergence a Dud?

☐ Bullish divergence fails to beat the market more often than it works. See Testing Divergence.

☐ Only bullish divergence works and only in a bull market. See Table 5.1.

☐ If the RSI indicator remains shallow during divergence, performance improves, but only in a bear market. See Table 5.2.

☐ Look for small M- or W-shaped turns beginning from the overbought or oversold regions. It is best if the right peak is below—or the right valley is above—the left one. See (7) Good Eggs: Indicator Failure Swings.

☐ Use the linear scale to look for flat bases on the weekly or monthly charts. See (8) Flat Base Entry Pattern.

☐ Area gaps appear in congestion regions on high volume, but price fills the gap quickly and continues consolidating. See Area Gaps.

☐ Breakaway gaps appear as price leaves a consolidation region on high volume. The gap does not close quickly. See Breakaway Gaps.

☐ Continuation gaps appear near the middle of a straight-line run, often on high volume. See Continuation Gaps.

☐ Exhaustion gaps appear at the end of trends, on high volume, and close quickly. See Exhaustion Gaps.

☐ See How to Trade Gaps for a list of trading tips.

☐ A violent reversal sometimes occurs after an exhaustion gap. See How to Trade Gaps.

☐ If the market hands you a gain, take it to the bank. See (10) The Never Lose Pattern: The Inverted Dead-Cat Bounce.

☐ If the S&P or Nasdaq futures make a big move, either higher or lower, expect the stock market to open accordingly. See (11) What Are the Futures Doing?

☐ After price jumps higher, if it closes at the high for the day, place a limit order to sell the next day at 1.38 percent above the close. See Table 5.3.

☐ Bullish tails appear at minor lows as price spikes below the adjacent price bars, but close near the high. They signal a move higher. See Table 5.4.

☐ Bearish tails appear at minor highs like a lone tree on a hill. They mean a downturn is coming. They are not as reliable as bullish tails. See Table 5.4.

☐ Price fails to make a lower low or higher high the day after a tall (twice the one-month average height) price bar at least 68 percent of the time. See Table 5.5.

☐ After a tall price bar, price shows a slight tendency to close lower the next day. See Table 5.5.

☐ Use ugly double bottoms to detect a change from bear to bull. See (15) Ugly Double Bottom: A Higher Bottom.

☐ When many stocks show pipe bottoms, look for a bounce leading to a second bottom. That second bottom may spell the end of the bear market. See (16) Bullish Chart Patterns Appear.

☐ When brokers downgrade stocks across the board and upgrade few, the end of the bear market could be near. See Table 5.6.

☐ If the S&P 500 index is down 50 percent from the high, it is near bottom. See (18) You Feel Like Selling Everything.

☐ Volume spikes at bear market bottoms. See (19) High Volume Bottom.

☐ When good news lifts the market and bad news has little effect, expect the end of a bear market. See (20) Bad News Moves Nothing, Good News Lifts Market.

☐ A partial rise predicts a downward breakout. A partial decline predicts an upward breakout. See (21) Getting in Early: Partial Rises and Declines.

☐ After an upward breakout from a chart pattern, holding a stock for up to three pattern widths tends to see the best gains in the shortest time. See Table 5.7.

☐ After a downward breakout from a chart pattern, shorting the stock for longer than two pattern widths gives little extra return for the risk involved. See Table 5.7.

☐ Price drops faster than it rises. See (23) Price Drops Faster than It Rises.

☐ Think of what price will do in the future by reflecting price movement around a peak or valley. See (24) Mirrors for Trend Prediction.

☐ Reflect the vertical distance across a trendline to help predict how far price will drop. See (25) Trendline Mirrors: Another Reflection.

☐ Avoid investing in stocks showing a price mountain. See (26) Avoid Price Mountains.

☐ On average, it can take more than five years for price to recover after a price mountain. See How Long to Summit a Price Mountain?

☐ When contemplating a trading decision, what would you tell your parents to do with a similar holding? See 14 Selling Tips You Need to Know.

☐ Use a stop loss order for short-term trades. See (27) Use Stops.

☐ At what price will the market tell me I am making a mistake? See (28) Sell When Wrong.

☐ If a stock makes an adverse or unexpected move, sell it. See (29) Sell on the Unexpected.

☐ If a stock drops 20 percent from a high, sell it. See (30) Sell on Trend Change.

☐ Sell a blue chip when it drops 10 percent from a peak. See (31) Sell Blue Chips 10 Percent Down.

☐ Understand your indicator tools so that when they say sell, you believe it. See (32) Indicator Says Sell: Obey It.

☐ Overlay your indicators on the same price chart to see if they signal at the same time. Remove duplicates. See (32) Indicator Says Sell: Obey It.

☐ If you followed your trading rules, would you make more money? See (33) Follow Your Rules.

☐ Sell if a bearish chart pattern confirms as valid. See (34) Sell on Confirmation of Bearish Pattern.

☐ Use the measure rule to gauge how far price is likely to move. See (35) Sell on Price Target.

☐ Convert the predicted rise or decline into a percentage to see if the move makes sense. See (35) Sell on Price Target.

☐ If price closes below support, then determine where price might stop declining. If support is nearby, then expect a pullback. See (36) Sell on Piercing Support.

☐ Watch the behavior of stocks in the same industry as a clue to weakness or strength. See (37) Sell on Industry Weakness.

☐ Look for deteriorating fundamentals, such as overhead increasing faster than sales or profits. See (38) Weak Fundamentals.

☐ Sell on hype. When everyone is talking about the latest gizmo, then the peak is near. Sell. See (39) Sell on Hype.

☐ When contemplating a sale, ask, what would Tom do? See (40) What Would Tom Do?

☐ A three-point channel suggests where price could go. See (41) Drawing Three-Point Channels.

☐ Use Andrews pitchfork to determine price trends. See (42) Andrews Pitchfork.

☐ Throwbacks occur about half the time in chart patterns, returning the stock back to the breakout price within a month. See (43) Beware Throwbacks and Pullbacks.

☐ A pullback occurs just over half the time, returning the stock back to the trendline boundary or breakout price before it resumes its downward move. See (43) Beware Throwbacks and Pullbacks.

☐ Price formed a peak or valley within a few days of a triangle apex 75 percent of the time. See Visual Test.

☐ Price changed direction 60 percent of the time within a few days of the triangle apex. See Automated Test.

☐ The average distance from peak or valley to the triangle apex is 3.6 days. See Math Test.

☐ Volume tends to hit very low levels a few days before the breakout. See (45) Volume Preceding the Breakout.

CHAPTER 6: FINDING AND FIXING WHAT IS WRONG

☐ Increase odds of success and profitability by trading with the trend. See What Was the Market Behavior?

☐ Did the trade direction (long in an up market, short in a down market) agree with the market direction? See What Was The Market Behavior?

☐ Use a moving average to help determine the market trend. See What Was The Market Behavior?

☐ Is overhead resistance nearby that might limit a move? See What Was The Market Behavior?

☐ Compare the trend of stocks in the same industry or use an ETF/sector fund that represents the industry. See Was the Industry Trending?

☐ Compare your industry ETF or sector fund with the general market and buy industries that are rising faster than the market (showing better relative strength). See Was the Industry Trending?

☐ Improve profitability by trading with the market and industry trends. See Does a Rising Tide Really Lift All Boats?

☐ The industry trend is more important than the market trend. See Table 6.1.

☐ Did you enter the trade too early, too late, or just right? See Early Entry.

☐ Do not chase a stock. If you cannot buy within 5 percent of the breakout (optimum entry price), then skip the trade or wait for a retrace. See Late Entry.

☐ Holding a trade too long is worse than selling too early. See Table 6.2.

☐ Never fall in love with a stock. See Are All Entry Conditions Met?

☐ Is each trade properly capitalized? See Are All Entry Conditions Met?

☐ Be careful trading after a string of winners. The overconfidence could produce a big loss. See Overconfidence: My Worst Trades.

☐ Wait for all entry conditions to trigger before buying. See Overconfidence: My Worst Trades.

☐ Did you size each position properly? See Was the Position Size Proper?

☐ Was an initial stop used? See Was an Initial Stop Used?

☐ Was the stop positioned properly? See Was an Initial Stop Used?

☐ Did you ignore the stop or remove it? See Was an Initial Stop Used?

☐ Did you use a trailing stop? See Did You Exit Before the Stop?

☐ Was the trailing stop properly positioned? See Did You Exit Before the Stop?

☐ Did you exit before the stop triggered? See Did You Exit Before the Stop?

☐ Sometimes selling early is smart; just do not let it become a habit. See Did You Exit Before the Stop?

☐ Ignore the risk to reward ratio when you cannot accurately determine the reward. See What Was the Risk/Reward Ratio?

☐ For trades with profit targets, use a risk to reward ratio of 3 or 4 (or higher) to 1. See What Was the Risk/Reward Ratio?

☐ The reward must be high enough to compensate for losing trades.

☐ Does your trading plan allow for averaging up? See Did You Average Up?

☐ When you averaged up, was it a profitable move? See Did You Average Up?

☐ Only investors and position traders should average down, and only in rare situations. See Did You Average Down?

☐ If you average down, then do so only *once* and add no more than 50 percent of your initial investment. See Did You Average Down?

☐ Sell in May and go away. See Are You Buying Out of Season?

☐ Based on your trades, are certain months better for trading than others? See Are You Buying Out of Season?

☐ Use a trading checklist so that important items are not forgotten. See Trading Checklist.

Visual Appendix of Chart Patterns

Broadening Bottoms

Broadening Formations,
Right-Angled and Ascending

Broadening Formations,
Right-Angled and Descending

Broadening Tops

Broadening Wedges, Ascending

Broadening Wedges, Descending

Bump-and-Run Reversal
Bottoms

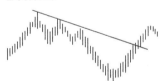

Bump-and-Run Reversal Tops

Cup with Handle

Cup with Handle, Inverted

Dead-Cat Bounce

Dead-Cat Bounce, Inverted

Diamond Bottoms

Diamond Tops

Double Bottoms, Adam & Adam

Double Bottoms, Adam & Eve

Double Bottoms, Eve & Adam

Double Bottoms, Eve & Eve

Double Tops, Adam & Adam

Double Tops, Adam & Eve

Double Tops, Eve & Adam

Double Tops, Eve & Eve

Flags

Flags, High and Tight

Gaps

Head-and-Shoulders Bottoms

Head-and-Shoulders Bottoms, Complex

Head-and-Shoulders Tops

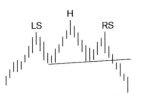

Head-and-Shoulders Tops, Complex

Horn Bottoms

Horn Tops

Island Reversals, Bottoms

Island Reversals, Tops

Islands, Long

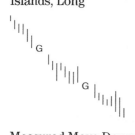

Measured Move Down

Measured Move Up

Pennants

Pipe Bottoms

Pipe Tops

Rectangle Bottoms

Rectangle Tops

Rounding Bottoms

Rounding Tops

Scallops, Ascending

Scallops, Ascending and Inverted

Scallops, Descending

Scallops, Descending and Inverted

Three Falling Peaks

Three Rising Valleys

Triangles, Ascending

Triangles, Descending

Triangles, Symmetrical

Triple Bottoms

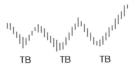

Triple Tops

Wedges, Falling

Wedges, Rising

Bibliography

Active Trader Staff. "Intraday Swing Extremes." *Active Trader* 12, no. 5 (May 2011).

Bandy, Howard. "Scaling Out as an Exit Technique." *Active Trader* 10, no. 9 (September 2009).

Bandy, Howard. "Scaling In as an Entry Technique." *Active Trader* 10, no. 10 (October 2009).

Bulkowski, Thomas. "A Trend Channel Trade." *Technical Analysis of Stocks & Commodities* 14, no. 4 (April 1996).

Bulkowski, Thomas. *Encyclopedia of Candlestick Charts*. Hoboken, NJ: John Wiley & Sons, 2008.

Bulkowski, Thomas. *Encyclopedia of Chart Patterns*, 2nd ed. Hoboken, NJ: John Wiley & Sons, 2005.

Bulkowski, Thomas. *Getting Started in Chart Patterns*. Hoboken, NJ: John Wiley & Sons, 2006.

Bulkowski, Thomas. *Trading Classic Chart Patterns*. Hoboken, NJ: John Wiley & Sons, 2002.

Bulkowski, Thomas. *Visual Guide to Chart Patterns*. Hoboken, NJ: John Wiley & Sons, 2013.

De Bondt, Werner F. M., and Richard H. Thaler. "Further Evidence on Investor Overreaction and Stock Market Seasonality." *Journal of Finance 42*, no. 3 (July 1987).

Desai, H., and P. Jain. "Long-Run Common Stock Returns Following Stock Splits and Reverse Splits." *Journal of Business* (1997).

Fama, Eugene F., and Kenneth R. French. "The Cross-Section of Expected Stock Returns." *Journal of Finance* 47, no. 2 (June 1992).

Fama, Eugene F., Lawrence Fisher, Michael C. Jensen, and Richard Roll. "The Adjustment of Stock Prices to New Information." *International Economic Review* 10 (February 1969).

Farley, Alan S. *The Master Swing Trader*. New York: McGraw-Hill, 2001.

Fischer, Robert, and Jens Fischer. *Candlesticks, Fibonacci, and Chart Pattern Trading Tools*. Hoboken, NJ: John Wiley & Sons, 2003.

Fosback, Norman G. *Stock Market Logic: A Sophisticated Approach to Profits on Wall Street*. Fort Lauderdale, FL: The Institute for Econometric Research, 1976.

Frost, A. J., and Robert R. Prechter. Jr. *Elliott Wave Principle: Key to Market Behavior.* Chichester, England: John Wiley & Sons, 1999.

Garcia de Andoain, Carlos and Frank W. Bacon. "The Impact of Stock Split Announcements on Stock Price: A Test of Market Efficiency." *Proceedings of ASBBS* 16, no. 1 (2009).

Glass, Gary S. "Extensive Insider Accumulation as an Indicator of Near Term Stock Price Performance." PhD diss., Ohio State University, 1966.

Grinblatt, Mark S., Ronald W. Masulis, and Sheridan Titman. "The Valuation Effects of Stock Splits and Stock Dividends." *Journal of Financial Economics* (1984).

Guppy, Daryl. "Matching Money Management with Trade Risk." *Technical Analysis of Stocks & Commodities* 16, no. 5 (May 1998).

Guppy, Daryl. "Exploiting Positions with Money Management." *Technical Analysis of Stocks & Commodities* 17, no. 9 (September 1999).

Hall, Alvin D. *Getting Started in Stocks*, 3rd ed. New York: John Wiley & Sons, 1997.

How to Invest in Common Stocks. The Complete Guide to Using The Value Line Investment Survey. New York: Value Line Publishing, Inc., 2007.

Ikenberry, David, G. Rankine, and E. K. Stice. "What Do Stock Splits Really Signal?" *Journal of Financial and Qualitative Analysis* (1996).

Investopedia.com. "Keep Your Eyes on the ROE." www.investopedia.com/articles /fundamental/03/100103.asp.

Jaenisch, Ron. "The Andrews Line." *Technical Analysis of Stocks & Commodities* 14, no. 10 (October 1996).

Kaplan, Peter. "Finding the Value in Losses." *Stocks, Futures and Options,* September 2006.

Kaufman, Perry J. *A Short Course in Technical Trading.* Hoboken, NJ: John Wiley & Sons, 2003.

Knapp, Volker. "Top Stop Exit." *Active Trader* 9, no. 9 (September 2008).

Knapp, Volker. "Insider Buying." *Active Trader* 9, no. 10 (October 2008).

Knapp, Volker. "Insider Selling." *Active Trader* 9, no. 11 (November 2008).

Lakonishok, Josef, Andrei Shleifer, and Robert W. Vishny. "Contrarian Investment, Extrapolation, and Risk." *Journal of Finance* 49, no. 5 (December 1994).

Landry, Dave. "Trading Trend Transitions." *Active Trader* 11, no. 12 (December 2010).

Lynch, Peter, and John Rothchild. *One Up on Wall Street: How to Use What You Already Know to Make Money in the Market.* New York: Penguin Books, 1990.

Mamis, Justin, and Robert Mamis. *When to Sell: Inside Strategies for Stock-Market Profits.* New York: Cornerstone Library, 1977.

Martell, Terrence F., and Gwendolyn P. Webb. "The Performance of Stocks that Are Reverse Split." New York: Baruch College/The City University of New York, 2005.

McClure, Ben. "Keep Your Eyes on the ROE." www.Investopedia.com/articles /fundamental/03/100103.asp.

Nicholson, S. Francis. "Price-Earnings Ratios." *Financial Analysts Journal 16*, no. 4 (July–August 1960).

Nilsson, Peter. "Money Management Matrix." *Technical Analysis of Stocks & Commodities* 24, no. 13 (December 2006).

O'Hare, Patrick. "Looking for Bottoms in Individual Stocks." *Stocks, Futures & Options* 3, no. 5 (May 2004).

O'Higgins, Michael, and John Downes. *Beating the Dow*. New York: HarperCollins, 1992.

O'Shaughnessy, James. *What Works on Wall Street*. New York: McGraw-Hill, 1997.

Patel, Pankaj N., Souheang Yao, and Heath Barefoot. "High Yield, Low Payout." *Credit Suisse*, August 2006.

Pugliese, Fausto, "Daytrading Rule 1: No Overnights." *Technical Analysis of Stocks & Commodities* 30, no. 7 (June 2012).

Rogoff, Donald T. "The Forecasting Properties of Insider Transactions." PhD diss., Michigan State University, 1964.

Sperandeo, Victor, with Sullivan Brown. *Trader Vic—Methods of a Wall Street Master*. New York: John Wiley & Sons, 1991, 1993.

Stowell, Joseph. "Teacher, Trader Still Teaching: Joseph Stowell." *Technical Analysis of Stocks & Commodities* 13, no. 7 (July 1995).

Subach, Daniel. "Stock Analysis and Investing for the Small Investor." *Technical Analysis of Stocks & Commodities* 24, no. 13 (December 2006).

Tweedy, Browne Company LLC. "What Has Worked in Investing: Studies of Investment Approaches and Characteristics Associated with Exceptional Returns." Revised 2009.

Vakkur, Mark. "The Basics of Managing Money." *Technical Analysis of Stocks & Commodities* 15, no. 9 (September 1997).

Vakkur, Mark. "New Tricks with the Dogs of the Dow." *Technical Analysis of Stocks & Commodities* 15, no. 12 (December 1997).

Vince, Ralph. *The Handbook of Portfolio Mathematics: Formulas for Optimal Allocation & Leverage*. Hoboken, NJ: John Wiley & Sons, 2007.

Weinstein, Sam. *Stan Weinstein's Secrets for Profiting in Bull and Bear Markets*. New York: McGraw-Hill, 1988.

Wisdom, Gabriel. *Wisdom on Value Investing*. Hoboken, NJ: John Wiley & Sons, 2009.

OTHER SITES OF INTEREST

www.Activetradermag.com—website for *Active Trader* magazine.

www.ThePatternSite.com—Mr. Bulkowski's website.

www.traders.com—website for *Technical Analysis of Stocks & Commodities* magazine.

www.Yahoo.finance.com—a general finance website.

About the Author

Thomas Bulkowski is a successful investor with more than 30 years of experience trading stocks. He is also the author of the John Wiley & Sons titles:

- *Visual Guide to Chart Patterns*
- *Getting Started in Chart Patterns*
- *Trading Classic Chart Patterns*
- *Encyclopedia of Candlestick Charts*
- *Encyclopedia of Chart Patterns, Second Edition*
- *Evolution of a Trader: Fundamental Analysis and Position Trading*
- *Evolution of a Trader: Swing and Day Trading.*

Bulkowski is a frequent contributor to *Active Trader* and *Technical Analysis of Stocks & Commodities* magazines. Before earning enough from his investments to *retire* from his day job at age 36, Bulkowski was a hardware design engineer at Raytheon and a senior software engineer for Tandy Corporation.

His website and blog are at www.thepatternsite.com, where you can read over 500 articles and the latest research on chart patterns, candlesticks, event patterns, and other investment topics, for free, without registering.

Index

Printed and bound by CPI Group (UK) Ltd, Croydon, CR0 4YY

16/04/2025

14658451-0001